Mike Oakley was born and brought up in Dorset before moving to Bristol in the mid 1960s, where he worked in town and country planning until retiring in 1996. In recent years he has developed a keen interest in the history and role of railway stations and halts, particularly in the West Country. As a result, he has built up a substantial library of photographs of Somerset's stations, a selection of which are reproduced in this book. He is also the author of *Bristol Suburban* (1990), an illustrated account of the city's stations and halts and 'Discover Dorset' *Railway Stations* (2001).

Following page
Clutton (*see page 43*)

SOMERSET
RAILWAY STATIONS

Mike Oakley

THE DOVECOTE PRESS

Bath Spa. A view eastwards in the original station with overall roof.
An 1846 engraving by J. C. Bourne.

First published in 2002 by The Dovecote Press Ltd
Stanbridge, Wimborne, Dorset BH21 4JD

ISBN 1 904349 09 9

© Mike Oakley 2002

Mike Oakley has asserted his rights under the Copyright, Designs
and Patent Act 1988 to be identified as author of this work

Typeset in Monotype Sabon
Printed and bound by KHL Printing, Singapore

A CIP catalogue record for this book is available
from the British Library

1 3 5 7 9 8 6 4 2

CONTENTS

INTRODUCTION 8

THE STATIONS AND HALTS

The Main Lines and Branch Lines 11

The Weston, Clevedon & Portishead Light Railway 149

The West Somerset Mineral Railway 156

FURTHER READING 158

ACKNOWLEDGEMENTS 160

Cheddar. A train arriving on the opening day, 3rd August 1869.

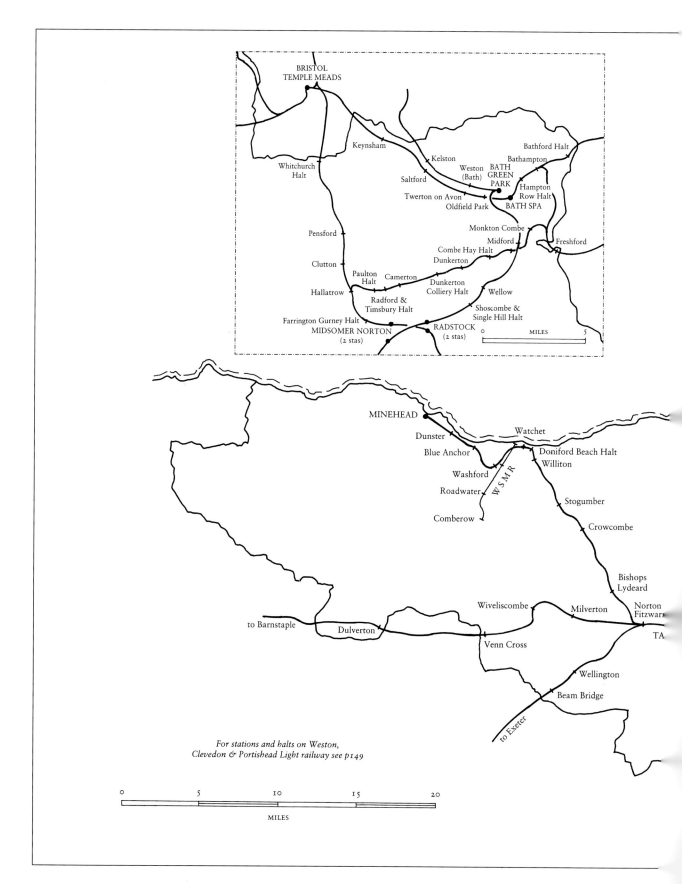

For stations and halts on Weston,
Clevedon & Portishead Light railway see p149

Somerset Stations and Halts

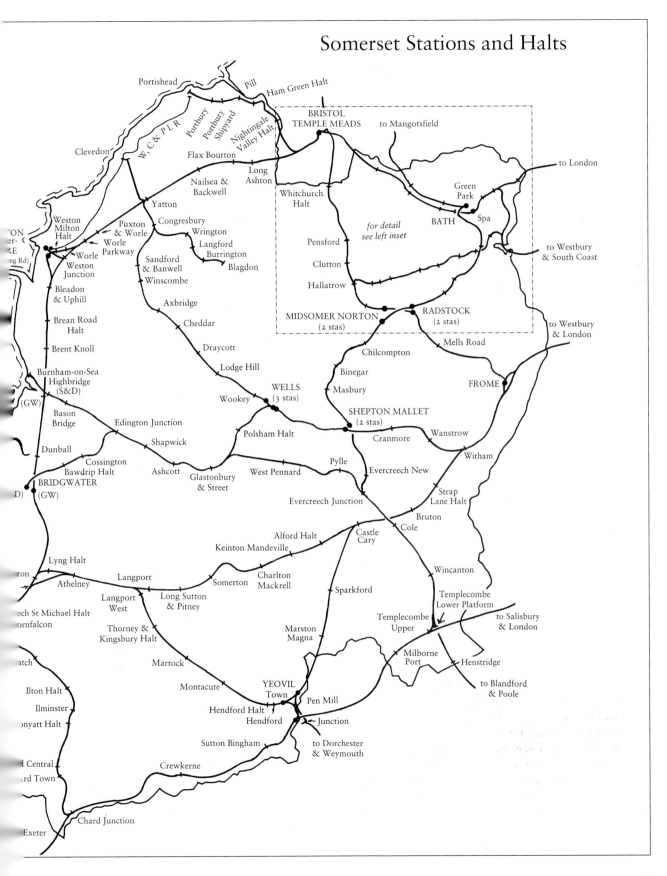

INTRODUCTION

Somerset changed for ever with the coming of the railway. The social and economic life of town and country was revolutionised with the greatly increased possibilities of travel and trading. The resorts of Portishead, Clevedon, Weston-super-Mare, Burnham-on-Sea and Minehead were now easily accessible by train from not only Bristol, but from London, the Midlands and the North. The rural community benefited from easier movement of commodities such as milk and livestock, and the local industries of glove making, footwear and paper found ready access to markets throughout the country.

The county's railway stations and halts played a significant role in these changes, with facilities developed to reflect the requirements of the various towns or villages, whether it was lengthy platforms to accommodate excursion trains, cattle pens for livestock on the way to market, or goods sheds for storage of products imported for the local community or for despatch from the local industries. The building style of the railway companies, often adapted to local conditions and materials, led to many railway related buildings becoming of architectural interest in their own right. The station master became a key figure in the town or village – responsible for the supervision of the station itself, the goods yard and local signal boxes. In many cases he was provided with a house, in some cases integrated within the station building, and sometimes even dwarfing the facilities provided for passengers!

This book relates to the geographical area of Somerset in 2002; stations or halts within the city of Bristol are not included. Many books have been published on the railways either in part, or the whole, of the county, though none focus specifically on the stations and halts. These accounts have been studied in the preparation of this book and further research undertaken, particularly where the published sources did not agree! All Somerset's stations and halts (or the site where they once stood) were visited during the early months of 2002. The accounts of each station and halt are in alphabetical order; in a few instances an introduction is given where the local railway history is particularly complicated (eg Wells, Yeovil). Where the term 'Halt' is included in the title it can be assumed that no facilities for the handling of goods were ever provided. Where the terms 'up' and 'down' platform are used they refer to the platform used for travel towards, or away, from London respectively.

Finally I have included two short sections and brief details relating to the stations and halts on the Weston, Clevedon & Portishead Light Railway and the West Somerset Mineral Railway, Many of the stations on the Weston, Clevedon and Portishead Light Railway had no platforms and only huts for shelter, and the four small stations on the West Somerset Mineral Railway only carried limited public passenger traffic.

The photographs reproduced are drawn from a large collection assembled from various sources over recent years. They have been selected primarily to illustrate significant and interesting features of the station or halt; thus only a few include engines or trains as their presence can obscure details of the station buildings!

THE RAILWAY NETWORK
1840-2002

The Bristol to Bath section of the Great Western Railway (GWR) Bristol to London line was the first railway to serve Somerset when it opened on 31st August 1840. The through line to the capital via Swindon and Reading opened just under a year later on 30th June 1841 with the completion of Box Tunnel, just over the border in Wiltshire.

Continuing the GWR London line into the West Country, the Bristol & Exeter Railway (B & E) opened in stages: from Bristol to Bridgwater (June 1841) and on to Taunton (July 1842), Beam Bridge near Wellington (May 1843) and Exeter (May 1844). Until 1849 the B & E line was leased to the GWR but from then it operated independently until

1876 when it was absorbed by the GWR.

The success of this new form of transport brought demands for new links to the Bristol – Taunton – Exeter line, in particular from resorts along the Bristol Channel coast. Branches were opened to Weston-super-Mare in 1841 (subsequently replaced by a loop line in 1884), and to Clevedon (1847), Portishead (1867), Watchet (1862)/Minehead (1874) and Barnstaple (Devon) via Wiveliscombe (1873). Inland links from the GWR line also opened from Taunton to Yeovil (1853) and Chard (1866)

A second through route from London to the West Country opened along Somerset's southern boundary in 1859/1860 with the Salisbury & Yeovil Railway and London & South Western Railway lines from Salisbury to Yeovil and Exeter serving Templecombe, Yeovil and Crewkerne. A short branch north to Chard opened in 1863.

Two further important routes were key to the development of Somerset's railway network. Firstly the Channel to Channel link. In 1854 the Somerset Central Railway opened a line from Highbridge Wharf to Glastonbury – a westward extension was completed to Burnham-on-Sea four years later in 1858. With a further extension eastwards to Cole, near Bruton, in 1862, a connection was made with the Dorset Central Railway which was developing a line north from Poole on the Dorset coast. The two companies amalgamated to become the Somerset & Dorset (S & D) Railway and in 1863 a through route was completed from Poole on the English Channel to Burnham-on-Sea on the Bristol Channel, the fulfilment of a long standing transport ambition.

However, traffic generated did not live up to expectations. It was not until 1874, when the S & D extension to Bath over the Mendips from Evercreech Junction opened, that the potential was realised. Bath Green Park to Poole then became the most used section of the S & D Railway. Branches from the Highbridge to Glastonbury section opened to Wells in 1859 and southwards, via the independent Bridgwater Railway to Bridgwater, in 1890.

The second key route was the north-south Wilts, Somerset & Weymouth Railway leaving the GWR London - Bristol line west of Chippenham (Wilts). This opened first to Westbury (Wilts) in 1848 and then Frome (1850), Castle Cary (1856), Yeovil (1856) and Weymouth (Dorset) (1857). The Wilts, Somerset & Weymouth Railway was absorbed by the GWR on 14th March 1850. Another line leaving the Bristol - London route at Bathampton opened to Bradford-on-Avon (Wilts) in 1857 traversing the

north east fringe of Somerset, including Freshford. A number of settlements on the northern fringes of the county were also served by a branch line which left the Midland Railway's Bristol to Gloucester line at Mangotsfield (Glos) and ran south-east to Bath Green Park Station, opening in 1869.

Even with all the above through routes and associated branches, there were still significant areas of Somerset not served by the rail network. A further area was covered however, with the opening of the Bristol & North Somerset Railway southwards from Bristol through Pensford, Clutton and Hallatrow to Radstock in 1873. At Radstock it linked with a previously opened freight line from Frome with passenger services commencing between the two towns in 1875. The North Somerset Coalfield provided large volumes of freight and passenger traffic to the new line. Also serving the coalfield area, a line opened eastwards from Hallatrow firstly to Camerton in 1882 and on through the Cam Valley (1910) to Limpley Stoke on the Bathampton to Westbury line.

A further east-west link along the southern slopes of the Mendip Hills came with the East Somerset Railway from Witham (on the Wilts, Somerset & Weymouth Railway) to Shepton Mallet (1858) and Wells (1862). The route linked to the Cheddar Valley & Yatton Railway from Yatton (on the GWR Bristol – Taunton – Exeter line) which reached Cheddar in 1869 and Wells in 1870. Wells now became the focal point of lines built by three different railway companies; a detailed account of the three stations and the links between them is set out in an introduction to the Wells section of the book. At the western end of the Cheddar Valley & Yatton Railway, a branch line from Congresbury to Blagdon (the Wrington Vale Light Railway) opened in 1901.

The last significant development of the Somerset railway network came in 1906 with the opening of the Castle Cary to Cogland Junction (on the Bristol - Taunton GWR line) section of the GWR southern cut-off route. Together with a new section of line in Wiltshire this provided a more direct GWR route to Taunton and the West Country via Newbury and Westbury rather than the longer northern route via Swindon, Bath and Bristol.

To complete the picture of lines in Somerset opening for passenger traffic, note must be made of the West Somerset Mineral Railway opened for a short time to passengers from Comberow to Watchet in 1865 and the Weston, Clevedon & Portishead Light Railway opening from Weston-super-Mare to Clevedon in 1897 and on to Portishead in 1907.

Many of the above lines subsequently closed to passenger and freight traffic. The principal closures (dates refer to closure to passenger services) were: Cam Valley line (1925), Wrington Vale (1931), Weston, Clevedon & Portishead Light Railway (1941), Wells and Burnham-on-Sea branches of the S & D (1951), Bridgwater branch of the S & D (1952), Bristol to Radstock and Frome (1959), Taunton to Chard Junction (1962), Yatton to Witham (1963), Taunton to Yeovil (1964), Portishead branch (1964), Mangotsfield – Bath Green Park – Evercreech Junction – Poole (1966), Evercreech Junction – Highbridge (1966), Barnstaple line (1966), Clevedon branch (1966) and Minehead line (1971).

Between 1976 and 1979, the West Somerset Railway reopened the line between Bishops Lydeard and Minehead; the East Somerset Railway also reopened a section of line west of Cranmore in 1980.

Above Alford Halt. Looking north east towards Castle Cary. No platform ramps at the far end.

Below Ashcott. Passengers waiting on the original wooden platform. The waiting room/booking office is beyond the station agent's house.

THE STATIONS AND HALTS

THE MAIN LINES AND BRANCH LINES

ALFORD HALT

OPENED: 21st July 1905 (on the Castle Cary - Charlton Mackrell section of the GWR cut off route Castle Cary - Cogland Junction, originally opened through this site 1st July 1905).

CLOSED: 10th September 1962. (with withdrawal of local passenger service between Castle Cary and Taunton).

Sited south of Alford village, the halt was one of three stations/halts opened on the first section of the GWR Castle Cary - Cogland Junction cut-off route. Unusually ramps were only constructed at the western end of the platforms. Illumination came from three lamp posts on each platform and any inter-platform movements were via footpaths up to a farm access road bridge to the west of the halt.

A private siding was in use off the down side to the east of the halt from 15th September 1940 until 8th April 1962. The siding gave access to an extensive War Department Depot that included thirteen sidings; access to the siding was controlled by a signal box only opened as required. No line-side trace of the halt can now be seen, though railings alongside the footpath to the platform on the down side are clearly visible.

ASHCOTT

OPENED: July 1856 (on the Highbridge Wharf - Glastonbury section of the Somerset Central Railway originally opened through this site in 1854).

CLOSED: Passengers - 7th March 1966 (with closure of the Evercreech Junction - Highbridge line to passenger traffic).

Goods - 13th July 1964.

This small station was sited on the east side of the level crossing on the road that links Ashcott (two miles to the south) with Meare (one mile to the north). Opening as Ashcott and Meare in July 1856,

it was re-named Ashcott in 1876, although the name boards continued to carry both names well into the twentieth century. The original wooden platform on the north side of the single track line was replaced by a concrete structure in the 1920s. No facilities were provided on either of these platforms. The booking office and waiting room were adjacent to the red brick station agent's house which was close to the Ashcott - Meare road at the west end of the platform. A single siding served a small goods yard on the north side of the line west of the level crossing. Ashcott and Shapwick, the next station along the line, were important for the movement of peat from the Somerset Levels. The yard junction was operated by a ground frame in a hut close to the level crossing gates.

Following demolition of the station house, a new bungalow was built on the site by a former porter at the station. The small building that housed the waiting room and booking office_appears to have survived, albeit with alterations, and is now in use for storage. Small portions of the base of the platform supports can also be traced alongside the track that runs in front of the new bungalow. Finally the two level crossing gate posts on the east side of the road still stand.

ATHELNEY

OPENED: Passengers - 1st October 1853 (with the opening to passenger traffic of the Durston - Hendford (Yeovil) branch from the Bristol & Exeter Railway).

Goods - 26th October 1853 (with the opening of the branch to goods traffic).

CLOSED: Passengers - 15th June 1964 (with the closure of the Durston - Yeovil line).

Goods - 6th July 1964.

Sited in the settlement of Athelney on the Somerset Levels on the east side of the Burrowbridge to North Curry road, the station originally opened on the

Athelney. The main station building on the down platform. 8th December 1963.

Durston to Yeovil branch. At this stage there was a platform on the north side of the single track and a goods loop on the south side. Its role was enhanced in 1906 when this section of the line was incorporated into the Cogland Junction to Castle Cary GWR cut-off route and the station was rebuilt on the now double track line. The main 1908 wooden building was sited at the west end of the down platform, both platforms being provided with a wooden shelter. Passenger numbers reached a peak in 1923 when 10,953 tickets were issued.

An original 1881 signal box on the north side, near the level crossing was used until 1906. A new box came into operation on the opposite side, also adjacent to the level crossing. This closed on 5th April 1986. It was dismantled in November 1989 and re-erected at Staverton on the South Devon Railway.

The station master's house, which survives today as Old Station House, stood close to the level crossing on the down side, while a short row of railway cottages with typical B & E style gable ends also remains. There is no trace of the actual station buildings on the site where Paddington - West Country trains now thunder through the automatic gates.

AXBRIDGE

OPENED: 3rd August 1869 (with the opening of the Yatton-Cheddar section of the Cheddar Valley & Yatton Railway)

CLOSED: Passengers - 9th September 1963 (with the closure of the Yatton - Witham line to passenger traffic).
Goods - 10th June 1963.

The station was sited on a ledge cut into the foothills of the Mendips, north of, and immediately above, Axbridge church and village. In common with others on this line it was an attractive stone-built station, typical of West Country branch line stations built in the mid-Victorian era.

The main buildings, on the up (village) side were of local Mendip stone with typical B & E features which included decorative barge boards, the station name carved in stone on the name board, and roofs of red tiles with alternating bands of plain and patterned tiles (generally six courses of saw-tooth pattern and four of plain). Ridge tiles were surmounted by a small cruciform motif.

The up side approach road was at the end of Station Road, which wound up a gentle incline from the village below. This road also served a large goods shed on which down pipes bearing the date 1869 can still be seen today. Pedestrian access to the station was via a footpath leading up through Axbridge churchyard, and the footbridge at the western end extended north carrying the path to Fry's Hill.

Axbridge. The principal buildings on the up side looking west. The foreground canopy provided cover for goods, mainly strawberries during the summer season.

A waiting shelter stood on the down side platform and the station master's house, also on the down side, was beyond the east end of the station. An old B & E signal box on the down platform was replaced by a new box off the east end of the same platform on 14th July 1907.

The handling of strawberries was a major trade throughout the station's life. Passenger ticket sales were high early in the twentieth century (22,971 in 1903) but by 1933 they had dropped to 2,683.

The A371 Axbridge by-pass now runs along the old track bed, immediately next to the buildings. The former station is in excellent condition and in use as Axbridge Youth Centre; the original B & E decorative barge boards are well preserved. The goods shed, including canopy, remains and is in industrial use. The station master's house is still used as a residence but cut off from the station site on the north side of the by-pass.

BASON BRIDGE

OPENED: July 1856 (on the Highbridge Wharf - Glastonbury section of the Somerset Central Railway originally opened through this site in 1854).

CLOSED: Passengers - 7th March 1966 (with closure of the Evercreech Junction - Highbridge line to passenger traffic).
Goods - 10th June 1963 (except siding to local creamery, closed 2nd October 1972).

Opening some two years after the Somerset Central Railway from Highbridge Wharf to Glastonbury, Bason Bridge was a one platform station on the north side of the single track, west of a level crossing over

Bason Bridge. An arrival from the Highbridge direction on 29th August 1964.

the B3141 Highbridge to East Huntspill road. The largely wooden buildings, with small fretted canopies and awnings, incorporated the booking office and waiting facilities. In front of these buildings the platform was narrow. A gentlemen's toilet was provided in a small separate building at the west end of the buildings. The crossing gates were controlled by a ground frame housed within a hut opposite the eastern end of the platform. A station master's house, constructed in 1901, was a little to the west of the station on a narrow site between the railway and the River Brue which flows east-west parallel to, and south of, the line. Much of the freight traffic at Bason Bridge was linked with milk, particularly after the opening, in 1909, of a large milk factory north east of the level crossing. In 1928 the station had no less than six staff; the station master, two clerks, two porters/shunters and a junior porter.

Following closure in 1966, the station was demolished in November 1968. However milk traffic continued from the factory until 2nd October 1972. The construction of the M5 motorway a mile and a half to the west precipitated the end of rail traffic to Bason Bridge. The factory itself did not close until 1987, being then used for a variety of industrial uses. Today the platform survives, hidden beneath a mass of undergrowth and brambles; the rear wall can be seen.

BATH GREEN PARK

OPENED: 4th August 1869 (as terminus of the Mangotsfield (Glos) - Bath branch from the Bristol - Gloucester line).

CLOSED: Passengers - 7th March 1966 (with closure of the Bath Green Park - Poole line to passenger traffic).
Goods - 31st May 1971.

The terminus station of the Midland Railway's branch from the Bristol - Gloucester and Birmingham line at Mangotsfield was sited on the banks of the River Avon. The station's development necessitated the demolition of nine Georgian terraced houses in Seymour Street.

The Bath terminus was, with the exception of the train shed, designed by J.H. Sanders who, together with the engineers Messrs Allport Junior and Wilson also designed other associated buildings. These included the goods station to the west of the new terminus, on the other side of the river, and the Midland Road bridge. The main station building was

constructed by Charles Humphries of Derby following acceptance of a tender for £9539. The contract for the erection of the train shed, designed by J.S. Crossley, was let separately to Messrs Hardyside and Co. of Derby whose price of £6,086 was in fact the lowest of only two tenders received.

The overall building was and is still today, very impressive. Marcus Binney in his classic book, *Railway Architecture*, says 'Perhaps the Queen of railway stations, certainly one of the best in the provinces for restrained elegance in the mid Victorian period, was Green Park in Bath . . . the forebuilding is impeccably Bath Georgian, long out of its time; through it one enters a train shed which, although designed without embellishment, is one of the most effective of its kind with its segmented ribs arising from plain octagonal columns, the roof structure itself resting tent-like, tangentially to the ribs.'

Appropriately the station was built in Bath stone, the fully glazed roof covered half of the platform length. Four lines were under the train shed but only the outer two faced onto platforms.

For some years it was claimed that the station was not ready for use with the opening of the line from Mangotsfield on 5th August 1869 and that until 7th May 1870 a temporary terminus was used on the west side of the river. However further research has concluded that the station, though far from complete, was used from the opening date. The *Bath Chronicle* of 5th August 1869 stated 'Much is yet to be done to render the station complete . . . the station is a very handsome one, both platforms being 450 ft long and covered for a distance of 220 ft. The roof, the span of which is 66 ft, is painted in vermilion, chocolate and white.'

Completion of the station and other facilities continued well into 1870, including the erection of stables fronting Green Park Mews, the Midland Railway Company providing its own horses for parcels and goods delivery and collection.

In March 1870 the local paper reported that 'the untidy space between the station's cross platform and the buffers had been filled in with earth in which evergreens and flowers have been planted,

Opposite page top Bath Green Park. The fine front elevation in the late 19th century.

Opposite page bottom Bath Green Park. Activity on the departure platform. Note the fine glazing in the west end of the roof.

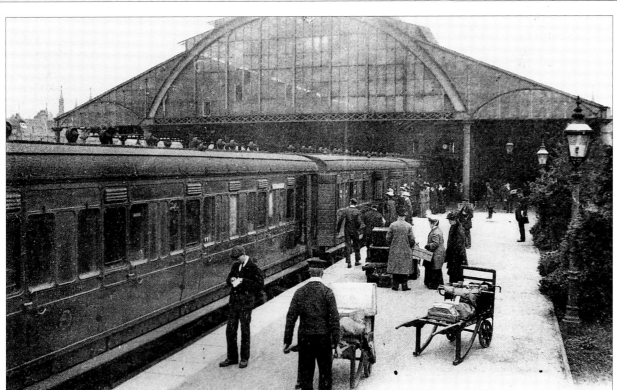

interspersed with ornamental rock-work'.

The original station changed in layout very little during its lifetime. It basically comprised an arrival platform (north side) with a covered area behind the west end for road carriage traffic, a departure platform (south side), a cross platform at right angles to the main platforms behind the buffers, a main booking hall, various waiting rooms (1st Class, 2nd Class, 3rd Class – including rooms specially for Ladies and Gentlemen) refreshment rooms (on the departure platform), toilets, station master's offices and accommodation, store rooms and last, but not least, a room for foot warmers. A large parcels office was sited on the arrival platform and beyond the end of this platform was a separate bonded warehouse. The last enabled goods wagons carrying bonded merchandise to be shunted into a secure building; it also provided facilities for casks of whisky and other spirits to be lowered by crane down to the station cellars. Vaults below the station platforms provided large areas for storage of the bounded goods which were transported through the vaults on small wagons running on rails in the cellar floors.

Even by April 1870 the volume of passenger traffic was rapidly increasing and both platforms were extended right up to the river bridge - the extra length required especially for summer excursion trains. The numbers of these markedly increased after the significant date of 20th July 1874 when trains of the S & D first used the station via its newly completed Bath extension over the Mendips from Evercreech Junction. Bath Green Park was now on a through route from the Midlands and North to the south coast. From 1910 a through train ran from Manchester to Bournemouth - in 1927 this became the 'Pines Express'.

Increased competition from cars, buses and locally the trams, began to make inroads into passenger traffic levels between the two World Wars. Some improvements and renovations were undertaken in 1938. Though there was less passenger traffic during the Second World War, increased military movements on the north/south route brought more trains through the station with the station traders benefiting from the stop for train reversal. The Baedeker raids over Bath in April 1942 brought significant damage around the Green Park area but fortunately not to the station itself. However, blast damage resulted in the loss of glass in much of the train shed and this was not replaced until the more recent renovation of the building after closure.

Post-war, local and through traffic revived and there were major holiday train movements in the late 1940s and early 1950s. Often twenty holiday expresses passed through on a summer Saturday. In 1954 a public address system was installed for the first time, initially for summer only and then permanently. The long stop necessary in order to attach fresh engines meant that refreshment rooms at the station were very busy and luncheon baskets were often provided for passengers on the 'Pines Express'. It was only on 18th June 1951 that the suffix Green Park was officially added, prior to this the name Queen Square had been unofficially used.

By the early 1960s use of the station had declined and through trains were withdrawn and transferred to other north/south routes. The last 'Pines Express' via Bath ran on 8th September 1962. Only local services on the S & D line and to Bristol used the station and with the closure of the complete Bath to Poole line to passenger traffic on 7th March 1966, Bath Green Park closed after 97 years.

It is ironic that after its closure the station became of greater interest to the public with the prolonged and complicated story of its possible demolition and subsequent renovation. After closure in 1966 the station fabric began to deteriorate rapidly; the buildings suffered damage and decay, not assisted by the roof lead being stolen. However, in November 1971 it was designated a Grade II listed building and a year later Bath City Council purchased the whole site and put in hand a number of urgent repairs to halt further deterioration.

During the following seven years various schemes were put forward for the site with, at one point, the City Council supporting an hotel scheme which could have involved the demolition of the train shed. Eventually in October 1979 Bath City Council supported an agreement between British Railways Board and J. Sainsbury for the leasing of the site with planning permission for a major supermarket. This scheme included the restoration of the whole complex but the bonded warehouse was not retained. Restoration commenced in earnest in 1981 and with some £1.5 million spent on the work Green Park was formally opened by H.R.H. Princess Margaret on 1st December 1982.

Today the Sainsbury's supermarket, with a more recent extension, and Homebase, occupy much of the site with the latter on the former goods yard and engine shed west of the river. Road names in the surrounding area serve as reminders of the past railway history: Pines Way, Stainer Road, Beale Road and also the name of the famous photographer and

Bath Spa. The northern frontage in about 1886. Tracks of the horse drawn trams in the foreground.

historian of the S & D Railway, Ivo Peters Road.

The building is now well used with the main booking hall occupied by the Green Park Brasserie. Many of the former offices and rooms are still as they were constructed, and are in use by a number of retail outlets and offices. Half of the train shed covers car parking whilst the other half is boarded over and used for local events and exhibitions. The original station finger board post sited on the cross platform is now preserved in the Somerset & Dorset Railway Trust's museum at Washford. The vaults under the departure platform contain the offices of the local environmental group, 'Envolve'.

BATH SPA

OPENED: 31st August 1840 (as the terminus of the Bristol Temple Meads - Bath section of the GWR Bristol - London line).

CLOSED: Passengers - remains open for services on the Bristol - London and Bristol - Southampton/ Weymouth lines.
Goods - May 1967 (depot). Open for full load traffic until 31st December 1980.

The GWR Bristol - London route via Box Tunnel opened throughout on 30th June 1841, but in the previous year the section from Bristol to Bath had been completed, terminating at Bath Spa Station. The suffix Spa was not officially added until 1949. Severe weather and flooding in the winter of 1839/40 had impeded building work and the station was far from finished at its opening. By the following year, however, the *Bath Chronicle* was reporting 'the noble structure is rapidly progressing . . . the building will form a very striking object when it is finished and will not only be a great ornament in the locality in which it is situated but it will also be worthy of the stupendous undertaking with which it is connected'. By the opening of the through route to London in June, the station was 'practically finished'.

The station (now Grade II listed) was built with the railway at first floor level, the tracks on either side being carried on high bridges over the winding River Avon. An engine shed and goods depot, the latter at right angles to the main line and accessed by turntable (as at Temple Meads, Bristol) were also squeezed into the limited available space. At ground level were stores and subways for passengers, carriages and luggage. The land for the station had been leased from Lord Manvers on 30th December 1837, with the GWR agreeing to construct and maintain roads in the station locality (eg Manvers Street and Dorchester Street).

The imposing north side (and main entrance) of the building, facing the city, was of asymmetrical design

Bath Spa. The southern down-side entrance in about 1925. The fine canopy has now gone.

with three Jacobean style gables and a central oriel window. The central gable lost its original pinnacle in 1931 and gained a clock. The walls were curved, providing an impressive sweep for carriages, and a canopy above the entrance allowed passengers to alight in the dry. This was originally a glazed timber construction but was replaced in the 1890s re-build. In 1845 an additional eastern wing was built and a further later extension to the west on the up side in yellow brick contrasts with the Bath stone of the original 1840s buildings. The building adjacent to the down platform was simpler in style but it also had an exterior canopy to shelter passengers.

Until 1897 the two platforms and four broad gauge tracks between them were covered by a train shed. Of 40 ft span, the roof was supported at the side by 26 large iron columns placed within 4 ft of the platform edge, thus giving little room for passenger movements when the train doors opened (*see engraving on page 4*).

Towards the end of the 19th century many complaints were made about the dilapidated state of the station. Except for the lengthening of the down platform to 400 ft and the up to 270 ft in about 1880, the facilities were almost unchanged from when originally built some forty years earlier. Some facilities were described as dangerous, in particular the narrow staircases to the platforms. The Mayor

spoke of the 'humiliation' he felt on escorting the Princess of Saxe-Weimar down the 'gloomy descents'. During a royal visit to the city in June 1889 a temporary platform was erected where the line passed through Sydney Gardens! Despite deputations and pleas from the City Council, little action was taken and the facilities were compared unfavourably to those at the Midland Railway's terminus station at Green Park.

Finally in February 1895 the GWR agreed that some £15,000 could be spent on station improvements. The up and down tracks were slewed to allow the platforms to be widened to give 8-9 ft between the platform edges and the columns. In 1897 an up-bay platform for four coaches was added; the main platforms were not only widened but they were also lengthened as far as possible without blocking access to stub sidings at the end of each platform. The same year the overall roof was removed despite a letter to the *Bath Chronicle* pleading for the retention of the 'fine train shed'. Long wide canopies now provided shelter over the platforms. Each platform was provided at this time with two hydraulic lifts, one for passengers and one for luggage; the passenger lifts were particularly well appointed with beech and pine panels. There were waiting rooms and refreshment rooms on both platforms, the up platform had two refreshment rooms, one for 1st Class passengers and the other for all classes. The facilities at the station remained basically the same for the next 50 years.

Bath Spa. The 'Merchant Venturer' from London on 28th August 1959. Note the elevated signal box.

From 1845 to 1936 an open girder bridge linked directly from platform level across the road to the Royal Station Hotel. Mrs Hughes, the proprietress, advertised her 'First Class Hotel for Families and Gentlemen' as 'Communicating by Private Bridge with the GWR Railway Station'. Another footbridge connected the down side approach with Widcombe High Street; built in 1877 it replaced an earlier suspension bridge which had collapsed early that year under the weight of excessive number of pedestrians.

Two original signal boxes dating from the 1840s, sited at each end of the station, were replaced in 1897 by one box situated unusually above the canopy of the down platform. This closed on 21st January 1968, with the major signalling scheme in the Bristol/Bath area implemented at that time.

Substantial damage was caused by an air raid in April 1942, particularly to the down side platform and building and also to the goods depot. The damaged canopy on the south side was not replaced until after the War.

After the early concentration of goods facilities just west of the station on the up side, goods provision became largely separated from the main station site, being concentrated mainly in the Westmoreland Yard area in 1877, some quarter of a mile west of the station. Animals and equipment were brought in by

rail for the Bath and West Show, and in 1903 a special train of 21 wagons brought Buffalo Bill and his Wild West Show to Bath! The site of the original goods facilities is now used as a car park and the Westmoreland Yard goods shed, in use until 1967, is now used as offices.

The original goods yard sidings at the up (Bristol) end were finally removed in 1960 to allow an extension of the up platform towards Bristol. This platform was extended for use from nine to fifteen carriages and the down extended from eight to ten carriage lengths following the removal of sidings at the east end. Ironically soon after this, train lengths were more standardised and shortened so the full length of the 1960 extensions has been rarely used.

One of the centre tracks was taken out of use on 25th November 1962 whilst the up-bay and the remaining centre track were taken out from 31st March 1967. In 1962 entrance and exit facilities were withdrawn on the Widcombe side and the pedestrian subway was renewed; in 1965/66 the four original hydraulic lifts were removed and the luggage subway closed.

Today the station is in good condition with many of the original features now well restored. The refreshment rooms on the up platform are still in place and the original up and down platform waiting rooms continue in use. At its relatively central location in Bath the station continues to provide convenient rail services to London, Bristol, the West Country and the south coast.

Bathampton. The Weston-super-Mare – London express passing through the station on 6th June 1960.

BATHAMPTON

OPENED: 2nd February 1857 (as a junction station on the GWR main line with the opening of the Bathampton - Bradford Junction branch of the Wilts, Somerset & Weymouth Railway).

CLOSED: Passengers - 3rd October 1966.
    Goods - 10th June 1963.

Sited on the main GWR line from Bristol and Bath to London some three miles east of Bath, Bathampton Station was originally intended to act as an exchange station for passengers transferring between trains on the Limpley Stoke valley line to Bradford on Avon (opened on the same date as the station) and the main GWR line. In the event all trains using the Bradford on Avon line ran to and from Bath and the Bathampton interchange role never materialised.

The main building, at the end of the long station approach road running beside the church, was on the down line. The station master's house was on the left hand side of the road approaching the station. A fine covered footbridge with an attractive valence connected to the up platform, on which stood a shelter with a small canopy. The original signal box stood at the east end of the down platform but this was replaced on 21st September 1956 by a new box at the east end of the up platform. This second box closed on 17th August 1970.

Passenger traffic was good for some years - in 1903 35,117 tickets were issued; this figure had more than halved by 1933 to 16,801. By then bus services were providing stiff competition for Bathampton residents travelling to and from Bath.

Sidings to the timber mills on the inside of the curve to Bradford on Avon opened on 10th October 1922, but goods traffic was never of great importance. In 1963 goods traffic ceased altogether and from 4th January 1965 staffing was withdrawn and the station was downgraded to a halt, nearly two years before it closed. The buildings and platforms were subsequently demolished, in part with the remodelling of the track-work at the junction to allow faster passage of trains to Bradford on Avon, Westbury and the south coast.

Now the only significant remains are the station gate posts at the head of the approach road together with a broken ex GWR notice, 'Private Drive'. All traces of the station at the track side have gone. The station master's house remains in residential use, Station House.

BATHFORD HALT

OPENED: 18th March 1929 (on the Bath - Wootton Bassett section of the GWR Bristol - London line originally opened through this site in 1841).

CLOSED: 4th January 1965.

Sited on an embankment to the north of the village and close to the junction of the A4 and A363, the

halt was a late addition to passenger facilities on the GWR line. Concrete platforms (250 ft x 8 ft) with basic iron shelters were provided at an estimated cost of only £164. Lighting was originally by gas but later by electricity. No staff were ever based at the halt, supervision being undertaken from Bathampton. Tickets were available from a local agent in Bathford. After a life of just over thirty five years, the halt closed in 1965. Today remains of the two footpaths leading up to the halt from either side of the rail bridge give clues to the halt's former site but no trace can be seen at the track side.

BAWDRIP HALT

OPENED: 7th July 1923 (on the Bridgwater Railway originally opened through this site in 1890).

CLOSED: 1st December 1952 (with closure of the Bridgwater line to passenger traffic).

The halt was opened following a 182 signature petition, led by the local vicar. The petition argued that two hundred people lived in Bawdrip with no shops, that the bus service was inadequate, and that a railway line already passed through the village. A short Southern Railway style concrete platform, which accommodated just three coaches, was built on the south side of the line. Fares were set at 4½d single to Bridgwater, 1½d to Cossington and 6d to Edington. Within a year, passenger numbers had reached about two hundred a week, which the residents felt justified the provision of a shelter. A

Bathford Halt. A view east towards Box Tunnel on 19th August 1961.

further request was made and, in 1924, a concrete hut with asbestos roofing costing some £28 came into use. Seats were also provided. In the winter months two lamps would be lit and these would be put out by the guard on the last train.

No trace of the halt now remains. A section of the trackbed west of the halt now forms the garden for a bungalow named whimsically 'Essandee'. A stone wall that supported the trackbed at this point can be seen.

Bawdrip Halt. A local train from Bridgwater in 1932.

Binegar. Looking north east, with the main building to the right on the down platform.

BEAM BRIDGE

OPENED: 1st May 1843 (as a temporary terminus of the Bristol & Exeter Railway).

CLOSED: 1st May 1844 (with the opening of the further section of the Bristol & Exeter Railway to Exeter).

With Whiteball Tunnel on the Somerset/Devon border being incomplete and needing another year's work, the B & E Railway extended its line from Taunton through Wellington to a temporary terminus at Beam Bridge in 1843. Stage coaches carried passengers on to Exeter along what is now the A38. Beam Bridge was apparently a busy terminus, having a daily service of eight passenger and two freight trains until its closure a year later, when the line was opened through to Exeter. No illustration of Beam Bridge is known to exist.

BINEGAR

OPENED: 20th July 1874 (with the opening of the Bath extension of the Somerset & Dorset Railway from Evercreech Junction to Bath).

CLOSED: Passenger - 7th March 1966 (with closure of the Bath Green Park to Poole line to passenger traffic).
Goods - 10th June 1963.

Over 700 ft high on the Mendips, the station served the villages of Binegar and Gurney Slade. The main buildings on the down (Shepton Mallet) side of the line with the typical S & D angled canopy on pillar supports, incorporated both general and ladies' waiting rooms, a booking hall/office, the station master's office and toilet facilities. On the up platform stood a signal box and a stone built waiting shelter with slate roof.

Beyond, and south west of, the station on the down side were fairly extensive good facilities including large and small goods sheds, cattle pens and a loading dock. Freight facilities at the station were probably more important to the local community than those for passengers. Between the goods shed and the down platform were two semi-detached houses for the station master and signalman. The whole station site was well tended with attractive flower beds.

Oakhill Brewery, two miles away, operated a 2 ft 6 inch gauge railway to the station from 1904 until the outbreak of the First World War. The track was lifted in 1921.

There is now no trace of the station buildings or platform. A large house, 'The Beechings', now occupies the site and the former station master's and signalman's houses are in residential use, as is the converted large goods shed. A former hand operated crane from the goods shed has been salvaged and is now at the Washford premises of the Somerset & Dorset Railway Trust.

BISHOPS LYDEARD

OPENED: Passengers - 31st March 1862 (with the opening of the West Somerset Railway from Norton Junction to Watchet).
Goods - October 1862

CLOSED: Passengers - 4th January 1971 (with closure of the Norton Fitzwarren - Minehead line).
Goods - 6th July 1964 (except some private sidings).

REOPENED: Passengers - 9th June 1979 (as the southern terminus of the restored West Somerset Railway).

Opened as the first station on the West Somerset Railway from Norton Junction to Watchet, Bishops Lydeard was sited about half a mile south west of the village. It was built with only one platform, on the down side, and included the station building, a brick goods shed and the station master's house, the last at the south end of the station. The up platform with a waiting shelter, passing loop and signal box were added 44 years later, coming into use on 2nd July, 1906. The main goods facilities were on the down side with cattle pens to the south of the goods shed behind the platform. A further long siding behind the

Bishops Lydeard. A Taunton train waits at the up platform. The main building is on the down.

up platform served a coal depot and a corrugated iron hut acted as a store at the north end of the platform. In 1943 a siding was added to a Government Army Food Depot.

The station remained relatively unchanged throughout its GWR/British Rail life but with the decline of the line in the 1960s it became unstaffed with the closure of the signal box on 1st March 1970. Goods services were withdrawn in 1964 and passenger services in 1971.

Since the 1979 reopening of the station as the southern terminus of the restored West Somerset Railway, the original buildings have been restored in the style of a GWR branch line station and the signal box is now operational again. In 1992 a booking office opened in a small new building on the up side and four years later a new shop/café building with a canopy was developed adjacent to the old up side waiting room. The up platform was also extended at the Norton Fitzwarren end in order to accommodate an eleven coach train and lamp posts from the closed Tiverton Junction Station installed.

Behind the down platform the goods shed, having been lengthened at the south end, is now in use as the Gauge Museum, housing a model railway layout and items of Railwaymania amongst other exhibits of railway history. The original down side building is now the West Somerset Railway Association office. The building between this office and the goods shed was built in the late 1970s by members of the Taunton Model Railway Club and is used as a club room. When visited in spring 2002, a camping coach was sited to the south of the goods shed. Purchased in 1997 and originally sited at Crowcombe Heathfield, it provides overnight accommodation for volunteers working on the West Somerset Railway. A large water tank at the south end was bought from a nursery at Ilton and now serves as the water supply for the many steam locomotives in operation. The former station master's house remains.

With its growth as a terminus of the West Somerset Railway, car parking/toilet facilities were for some years a major problem This issue was tackled in 1997 with the development of a large new car park and toilet block on land close to and behind the up side. Throughout its life the station has always been renowned for its well kept gardens and in 2001 the station entered the Taunton in Bloom contest and was the winner of the Public Services Cup.

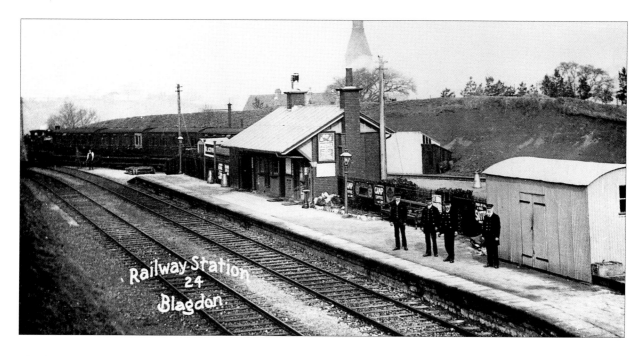

Blagdon. The staff posing at this small branch terminal station; the station building survives as part of a large house.

BLAGDON

OPENED: 4th December 1901 (with the opening of the Wrington Vale Light Railway from Congresbury to Blagdon).

CLOSED: Passengers - 14th September 1931 (with closure of the Wrington Vale Light Railway to passenger traffic).

Goods - 1st November 1950 (with closure to goods traffic of the Wrington - Blagdon section).

The country terminus of the Wrington Vale Light Railway, Blagdon Station was in a wide cutting close to Blagdon Lake but some half mile north of the village. More significant then the actual distance was the steep climb up Station Road to the village centre. This was always a deterrent for passengers, especially when bus services offered an alternative means of transport from the 1920s.

Blagdon Station was similar in style to those at Langford and Wrington. It was built in red brick and timber with a zinc roof and small canopy, with a platform 200 ft long and 2 ft 6 inches high. After its opening, a porters' room and stables at the Wrington end were also provided. At the east end of the platform was a typical corrugated iron parcels shed and, as at Langford Station, a cast iron gent's urinal beside the main building.

A small goods shed was provided in the goods yard behind the station building. As appropriate at the line's terminus, an engine was based at Blagdon until 31st March 1924. It is thought that a wooden engine shed had been in place until destroyed by fire in 1912 but no map or photographic evidence supports this fact.

Being the branch terminus, Blagdon was the focus of celebrations for the Railway's opening in 1901 and some 1500 passengers were carried that day. Local businesses closed, a ceremony was held in the Blagdon village club and dignitaries were entertained at the nearby Combe Lodge.

Throughout its life the station served the local community with both passenger and freight trains, though the distance from the village and the steep hill were deterrents. The number of passenger tickets issued fell from 9,419 in 1903 to 3,407 in 1923. As at other stations on the Wrington Vale Light Railway milk traffic was important. Between the Wars a camping coach was sited behind the platform at the Wrington end.

The former station building and platform are now well preserved in residential use; a large two storey house built behind the platform is linked to the building. The platform remains with the former trackbed laid out as a lawn. Old station lamps are also in place - one has the name Blagdon on the lamp and another GWR Station. The whole complex is appropriately called Little Halt.

Bleadon and Uphill. Buildings on the up side platform, including the small signal box. The central shelter and the station house behind are of B & E origin.

laid out as a garden, and the former station house, with extensions, is in residential use. A new road bridge has replaced the original whose abutments can still be seen.

BLEADON AND UPHILL

OPENED: 1871 (on the Bristol - Bridgwater section of the Bristol & Exeter Railway originally opened through this site in 1841).

CLOSED: 5th October 1964.

Opened in 1871 as Uphill, it was renamed a year later. Sited immediately south of the A370 overbridge south of Weston-super-Mare and close to the Bleadon Toll Gate, the principal buildings were on the up side wooden platform. A shelter in the centre of the platform, together with the station master's house, sited some 100 yds behind the up platform, were provided by the B & E Railway when the station opened in 1871. They both displayed good examples of B & E decorative barge boards. The GWR later provided further shelters at both ends of the platform. A cast iron gent's urinal was sited adjacent to the central shelter and a small signal box also stood on the platform. Shelter on the down platform was provided by a typical B & E wooden structure also with barge boards. The principal access to the station was to the up side, leading from the A370 and the road also provided access to the station house. The station was unstaffed from 2nd November 1959.

For some years after its closure, a small railway museum was located on the station site, on the up side of the line, but this closed by the 1980s. The station building was demolished in the early 1990s. Today the former museum site can still be identified,

BLUE ANCHOR

OPENED: 16th July 1874 (with the opening of the Minehead Railway from Watchet to Minehead).

CLOSED: Passengers - 4th January 1971 (with closure of the Norton Fitzwarren - Minehead line). Goods - 19th August 1963.

REOPENED: 28th March 1976 (with the reopening of the Minehead - Blue Anchor section of the restored West Somerset Railway).

Opened in 1874, on the coast a mile north east of the village of Carhampton, its first name was Blue Anchor Excursion Platform. This reflected the view of the directors of the Minehead Railway that the residents of Carhampton were unlikely to be the principal source of passengers, but rather future visitors to the beach. Excursion Platform in the name also indicated that the directors did not intend the facility to be open at all times, but only to serve visitors. The name changed for about a year to Bradley Gate before Blue Anchor was finally established as the station name. This was derived from the blue clay which was often deposited on anchors of boats sheltering in the bay.

When it opened, there was only one platform on a single line. Sited on the coast side, a small building provided shelter for passengers. Compared with the other stations on the Minehead Railway at Minehead, Dunster and Washford, the directors did

Blue Anchor. An early view east with the principal buildings on the up side (left).

not see fit to provide more than a basic structure to serve excursionists and the building cost only £350. A small canopy protected the entrance but today's position may not be the original. Although some historians believed the building to have been there before the arrival of the railway, it has now been concluded that the building was erected specifically for the station.

In January 1904, the GWR added a passing loop, a down platform with waiting room, a signal box and level crossing gates. On the up platform a ladies' room was built together with a shelter between this and the main station building. Gentlemen's toilets were provided at the side of the main building. The waiting shelter on the down platform is a substantial red and blue brick structure with solid walls some fifteen inches thick. The large canopy over the platform is supported by steel girders spanning the full width of the building and tied to metal straps running down the rear wall. This structure thus avoids the need for pillars on the platform to support the large canopy. The up platform is stone faced, the down platform brick faced; together with the loop they were both lengthened in February 1934.

The 1904 signal box not only controls the points for the loop and adjacent goods yard but also contains a large wheel operating the level crossing gates at the Minehead end. The goods yard, to the west of the gates was not opened until 1913.

Since its reopening on the West Somerset Railway, extensive renovation has taken place. On the up side the booking office has been restored using GWR fittings, including a cast iron barrier from the former Somerton Station. A new shelter built between the booking office and the ladies' room replaced the original which had been demolished due to its unsafe condition. The down side waiting room has also been restored and since 1985 has housed a small GWR museum run by the West Somerset Steam Railway Trust. It was opened to celebrate the 150th anniversary of the GWR. Also on the down platform adjacent to the level crossing is the former oil lamp shelter at Highbridge, now primarily used as a store; it can also be used as a shelter. The signal box is still in service, in particular the wheel continues to operate the level crossing gates, the only example now left in the West Country. Three 1914 vintage carriages on the site of the former goods yard, which closed in 1963, provide accommodation for volunteers working on the line. The station gardens, as for many years, are an attractive feature of this well restored small station.

BREAN ROAD HALT

OPENED: 17th June 1929 (on the Bristol - Bridgwater section of the Bristol & Exeter Railway originally opened through this site in 1841).

CLOSED: 2nd May 1955.

Located to the north of a bridge carrying a minor road east-west from Lympsham to Berrow and Brean, this halt was also described in some timetables as 'Brean Road for Brean Sands' or 'Lympsham Halt'. When originally authorised in

Brean Road Halt. Looking north towards Bristol. Note the different designs of the small shelters.

April 1929, it had been proposed to call it Brean Bridge Halt. Built at a cost of £1487, the up and down platforms, 400 ft by 8 ft, were both provided with small shelters, that on the up being of corrugated iron and on the down, of wood. Direct road and footpath access was provided to both platforms. Milk and general produce were carried as well as passengers using the halt to come to Berrow

Brent Knoll. Looking north towards Bristol, the principal buildings on the down side (right).

and Brean Sands though, as with many such halts with 'road' in the name, this entailed a long walk! Today there are no trackside remains but the access from the Lympsham side can be identified with old rail posts at the former roadside path entrance.

BRENT KNOLL

OPENED: 1875 (on the Bristol - Bridgwater section of the Bristol & Exeter Railway originally opened through this site in 1841).

CLOSED: Passengers - 4th January 1971.
  Goods - 6th June 1963.

The station was sited south of a road overbridge carrying a minor road from Brent Knoll, immediately to the east, to the coast road between Berrow and Burnham-on-Sea. The station and the village are named after the nearby isolated hill rising from the Somerset Levels.

The principal buildings were on the down side - these comprised a main wooden building with the booking facilities and a waiting room, an adjoining small wooden building to the north and a small extension on the south side incorporating the gentlemen's toilet. The main station access was on this down side. On the up platform stood a wooden waiting shelter and buildings on both platforms displayed good examples of the barge boards seen on stations on this former B & E line. The road bridge

Bridgwater. General view towards Bristol on 3rd July 1934.

provided the pedestrian link between the two platforms. A down refuge siding and signal box were added to the north of the road bridge in 1891; an up refuge siding was also provided to the south of the station.

Today no trackside remains can be seen. On the down side the station site can be identified at the end of the approach road from the east, a nearby cottage is called 'Journey's End'. On the up side an industrial building for high pressure cleaning equipment stands at the end of the former approach road. Brent Knoll became unstaffed as from 1st October 1964 and at its closure early in 1971 there was only one up train calling per day.

BRIDGWATER

OPENED: 14th June 1841 (as the terminus of the first section of the Bristol & Exeter Railway).

CLOSED: Passengers - remains open for services on the Bristol - Taunton - Exeter line.
Goods - November 1965 (The docks branch closed 2nd January 1967).

The station, to the east of the town centre, opened as the terminus of the first section of the B & E Railway from Bristol. The line opened to Taunton in 1842, Beam Bridge south of Wellington in 1843, and Exeter on 1st May 1844. The arrival of the railway was a further step in the town's development, the docks having opened a little earlier. On 26th September 1949 the suffix Central was added but was later dropped.

Bridgwater remains today as one of the oldest surviving stations of the B & E. It is a Grade II listed building, designed by Brunel, with a fine canopy over the entrance on the up side. There are large single storey buildings on both platforms. The up platform building has deep Georgian style windows below a cornice, a low pitched roof being largely hidden from view behind parapets. The platform canopies on both platforms are supported by decorated pillars.

In 1882 £3700 was spent on improvements to the station - the platforms were extended by 15 ft, glazed roofs were added, as were waiting rooms, and a fine new covered footbridge at the Bristol end. The platforms were further extended in 1904. The station's main offices have always been on the up (town) side where a glazed screen protects passengers at the south end of the building. A large shelter stands on the down platform. For many years a large corrugated building was sited to the south of the main building on the up side providing facilities for parcels and other goods. This is no longer there. The footbridge over the tracks at the south end is not a

railway bridge but provides a connection across the site for pedestrians, linking housing areas. A siding led for many years into and behind the south end of the up platform.

When the line continued to Taunton in 1842, the B & E Railway built a carriage and wagon works south of the station on the up side separated by a timber yard and brick yard from the station site. After a busy period this gradually fell into disuse.

A timber two track locomotive shed opened with the line at Bridgwater in June 1841 but was removed to Taunton a year later when the railway reached there in 1842. Bridgwater was then without a locomotive shed until 1893 when a 120 ft long outer bay of the carriage works was converted into a small locomotive depot. Locomotives were kept here which were used for shunting at the station, in the goods yards and at the nearby docks. The depot closed in July 1960. As activity at the carriage works declined, buildings were demolished and everything was removed by 1960 except for a number of carriage sidings adjoining the main line. One still remains. Sidings to the timber yard and brick works were removed in 1964.

Bridgwater's principal goods facilities, including a goods shed, were on the up side, north of the station. Sidings connected into the Corporation Market in 1935. Between the station and the goods yard a line crossed the town itself connecting to the dock system on the River Parrett. On the level, it crossed a number of roads and was the cause of many traffic hold-ups in the town. It passed close to Bridgwater North, the terminus station of the Bridgwater

Bridgwater. Station frontage on the up side 10th May 2002. Note the name embellished above the entrance.

Railway, a branch from the S & D. When this latter station closed in 1954, a link line was laid to connect the S & D yard to the GWR dock tracks.

On the down side of the main line there was only a goods loop which was taken out of use in March 1972. For some years a siding to the north also linked into the British Cellophane Company factory.

The last goods sidings were taken out of use at Bridgwater in 1965 and the docks branch and sidings closed in 1967. Facilities for the handling of waste containers from the nearby Hinkley Point Nuclear Power Station still continue in use today north west of the station; a short siding behind the up platform also remains.

The station is today served only by local Bristol - Taunton - Exeter trains. It is used not only by passengers coming to the town for business, education and shopping but also by visitors to the annual Bridgwater Carnival. Some refurbishment has taken place in recent years including a renovated booking hall and an improved forecourt and car park. However, the main buildings, still incorporating original B & E features, are not in prime condition. A new housing development has recently been undertaken adjacent to the down side building. Station House and Station Cottages remain to the west of the station itself but the former Railway Hotel has been replaced by modern commercial development.

BRIDGWATER NORTH (S & D)

OPENED: 21st July 1890 (as the terminus of the
Bridgwater Railway opened on that date).

CLOSED: Passengers - 1st December 1952 (with closure
of the Bridgwater line to passenger traffic).
Goods - 7th July 1962.

Bridgwater (S & D) opened in 1890 as the terminus
of the independent Bridgwater Railway, a line which
left the S & D Railway's Burnham-on-Sea -
Glastonbury - Evercreech Junction line at Edington
Junction, some five miles to the north east. From its
opening the Bridgwater Railway was leased by the
S & D and operated as part of its system. A suffix
North was added to the station name as from
26th September 1949.

Sited closer to the town centre than the GWR
station, opened nearly fifty years earlier, Bridgwater
North was basically a north-south aligned two bay
island platform with its principal building at right
angles across the buffer stops. The single platform,
some 300 ft long was, apart from a short tapered
section at the north end, 50 ft wide. Some 200 ft was
covered by a long canopy supported by ten pairs of
decorated columns. At its southern end the 20 ft
deep concourse between the end of the canopy and
the station building was covered by a fretted canopy
sloping back towards the building.

The main building itself, facing the town, was
attractive and well proportioned, the design showing
evidence of London & South Western Railway
influence. It was very different from other stations on
the S & D system, having been built by the
Bridgwater Railway. It was constructed in local red
brick with round headed sash windows on the main
frontage, a hipped and tiled roof and three chimneys.
A large central entrance/booking hall was flanked on
its western side by the ticket office and the station
master's office and on its eastern side were the

Above Bridgwater North. An August 1952 view down
the island platform to the main station building.

Left Bridgwater North. The fine terminal building at
right angles to the island platform and buffer stops.

parcels office, general waiting room, ladies' waiting room, porters room, stores and toilets. A ramp to a loading dock was sited close to the west side of the building and between the east of the building and the station master's house a wicket gate gave a second access to the station. Bridgwater served passengers from a wide area of central Somerset using the S & D, and was also used by a good number of excursion trains, particularly for the annual Bridgwater Carnival. It is recorded that such events attracted excursion trains from as far away as Bath.

A large goods yard, with a brick goods shed (60 ft x 21 ft) and goods office was sited to the west of the station. A range of facilities were available to handle commodities, including bricks, tiles and livestock. Further to the west was a 50 ft turntable and an engine shed (60 ft x 25 ft); the shed was roofed with corrugated iron in contrast to the gable roof of the goods shed. Extended in 1898 to accommodate two locomotives, it was nevertheless not used to accommodate locomotives overnight after 1922 and in 1928 it was leased to the local Co-operative Society as a store. When the line to Edington closed on 4th October 1954 a new spur line connected the S & D yard to the GWR docks branch, thus maintaining access to the yard, which remained in use until 7th July 1962. The docks branch finally closed on 2nd January 1967. A signal box, built in 1930, stood to the north of the station and west of the level crossing across The Drove. It replaced an earlier box east of the line.

After the station closed in 1952, the site was used for many years as a transport depot by British Road Services. The station building itself was demolished in August 1984 as was the former engine shed, in use as a store, in December 1985. The goods shed survived intact until July 1985 when it burnt down. The former station master's house, renovated in the mid 1980s also burnt down in 1988 and was demolished when work began on the development of a store for J. S. Sainsbury. The supermarket with associated car parks now covers much of the station site and goods yard and no remains of the station can be seen.

BRISTOL ROAD HALT

Weston, Clevedon & Portishead Light Railway (*see p 150*)

BROADSTONE HALT

Weston, Clevedon & Portishead Light Railway (*see p 150*)

Bruton. Looking north east towards Witham and Frome. Substantial buildings with canopies stand on both platforms.

BRUTON

OPENED: 1st September 1856 (with the opening of the Frome - Yeovil section of the Wilts, Somerset & Weymouth Railway).
CLOSED: Passengers - remains open for services on the Bristol - Weymouth line.
Goods - 5th April 1965.

Bruton was sited at one of the original crossing places on the then single track broad gauge line from Westbury and Frome to Yeovil. The passing loop was however rarely used, with most trains using the up (towards Frome) platform. Both up and down platforms had substantial stone buildings with small canopies. The two buildings were fairly comparable in size, unusual for stations on the Wilts, Somerset & Weymouth Railway. The up platform building on Station Road was, however, the larger and incorporated the usual offices. A large bay window at the Castle Cary end was a particular feature. The down platform building was only a large waiting shelter. An open iron footbridge, built in 1895, connected the two platforms. Bruton signal box (1877, enlarged 1909) was sited at the Castle Cary end of the down platform. Also at this end of the station, but on the up side, was a broad gauge goods shed, cattle dock/pens and a crane.

Carefully tended flower beds and neatly pruned bushes showed the pride taken for many years by Bruton staff in their station's appearance.

Passenger numbers were always relatively high, much being generated by the three public schools in the Bruton/Cole area (*see Cole*). In 1903 16,101 passenger tickets were issued, 1913 16,021, 1923 12,891 and 1933 10,970. Parcels traffic was high –

in 1903 20,329 parcels were forwarded and by 1933 this had risen to 27,377, no doubt much of this was connected with the schools. Staff numbers which had been only five in 1863, rose to nine in 1913 and eight throughout the 1930s.

By the 1960s decline had set in and Bruton was down-graded to a halt on 6th October 1969. The goods yard had closed over four years earlier. The signal box remained in operation until 7th December 1983. Today sections of old station railings and gates are still in place, as is the metal footbridge with concrete steps; remnants of the station gardens can also be seen. A pre-fabricated metal building is on the site of the former goods shed. The station remains open for limited passenger services but the buildings have been demolished and replaced by bus stop type shelters, now in poor condition.

BURNHAM-ON-SEA

OPENED: 3rd May 1858 (with the opening of the Highbridge - Burnham-on-Sea extension of the Somerset Central Railway).

CLOSED: Passengers - 29th October 1951 (with closure of the Highbridge - Burnham-on-Sea line to regular passenger traffic - some summer excursion trains continued until 8th September 1962).
Goods - 20th May 1963.

The station opened as Burnham in 1858 after the 1¾ mile extension of the Highbridge to Glastonbury Somerset Central Line had been completed. The suffix 'on-Sea' was added as from 12th July 1920.

The terminus station with an overall roof and small entrance canopy faced north onto a forecourt at the junction of High Street, Pier Street and Abingdon Street. Under the overall roof which gave the station a rather gloomy air, but provided shelter from the Bristol Channel winds, there was a general waiting room, a booking hall and office, a ladies' waiting room and parcels office. At a later date a 225 yd long concrete excursion platform was built to the south of the line. This was much longer than the original 95 yd platform that led into the train shed. To the north of the main building were sited the principal goods facilities including a red brick goods shed, a more impressive building than the station itself. At the east end of the platform stood a small four lever signal box which closed in 1960 and is now at the Somerset & Dorset Railway Trust's site at Washford.

The tracks ran through the train shed and continued westwards down an incline on to a pier into the Bristol Channel. The pier was used by shipping from some years including railway owned ferries to Cardiff. The line was too steep for locomotive haulage and trucks were hauled by wire ropes and capstans. It is not thought that passenger trains ever used the pier line west of the station.

Alongside, and to the south of the main station, a lifeboat station operated for some years up to 1930, a siding from the pier line was used to take the lifeboat down to the pier for launching. This use of the pier line continued for some years after other use of the line was discontinued. Even after its formal closure to passengers in 1951, special summer excursions trains still ran to the resort, the last running on 8th September 1962. Other traffic from Burnham-on-Sea included passengers connecting with GWR services at Highbridge and also workers travelling to the S & D works at Highbridge.

Today the station site and the trackbed towards Highbridge are used by the new road leading from Highbridge to the sea front. The station building itself was demolished by 1967. For many years from 1937 the former lifeboat station was used as a scout hut but it is now in use as a children's play centre. The nearby Somerset and Dorset Hotel, with appropriate sign-board, stands at the junction of High Street and Abingdon Street, serving as a reminder of earlier days.

Burrington. The 1907 stone building on the south side of the single track Wrington Vale Light Railway.

BURRINGTON

OPENED: Passengers - 4th December 1901 (with the opening of the Wrington Vale Light Railway).
Goods - 2nd July 1903.
CLOSED: Passengers - 14th September 1931 (with closure of the Wrington Vale Light Railway to passenger traffic).
Goods - 1st November 1950 (with closure to goods traffic of the Wrington - Blagdon section).

Situated in a cutting nearly one mile north west of the village, Burrington was at first only a small halt with a simple platform and small shelter on the south side of the line. A stone station building subsequently came into use as from 26th September 1907; with a wooden awning, it was the only station building on the Wrington Vale Light Railway to have recognisable GWR styles. The new platform was some 200 ft long and 2 ft 6 inches high. At the same time a fine station master's house was built just to the west of the station near the road bridge and also a small goods yard with a siding. The yard, including a weighbridge, handled both coal and local agricultural produce. Further improved facilities for the handling of milk came in October 1909. The yard remained fairly busy until the Wrington Vale Light Railway was closed to goods traffic in 1950.

Like other stations on the line, numbers were never high during its 30 year life as a passenger station; the number of tickets issued fell from 4,850 in 1913 to 2,106 in 1923. However for many years, even after

closure to regular passenger traffic, the station was used by annual excursion trains with passengers travelling to Burrington Combe.

Burrington Station was demolished in 1958, the cutting was filled in, and today it is difficult to identify the former trackbed alignment. The location of the former road bridge west of the station can be identified through a hump in the road; at this point the former station master's house continues in residential use appropriately called 'Station House'.

CADBURY ROAD HALT

Weston, Clevedon & Portishead Light Railway (see p 150)

CAMERTON

OPENED: Passengers - 1st April 1882 (with the opening of the Hallatrow - Camerton branch to passenger traffic).
Goods - 1st March 1882 (with opening of the branch to goods traffic).
CLOSED: Passengers - 21st September 1925 (with final closure of the Hallatrow - Limpley Stoke line to passenger traffic). Temporary closure to passenger traffic, originally as a war time measure - 22nd March 1915 - 9th July 1923.
Goods - 15th February 1951 (with closure of the Camerton - Limpley Stoke line).

Camerton Station originally opened in 1882 as the eastern terminus of the Bristol & North Somerset Railway's branch from Hallatrow. This fact explains why Camerton Station, although basic, was similar in design to other larger stations on the main Bristol

33

- Radstock line. Costing some £685, and of the William Clarke station design, the main building stood on the north of the line. It had a large fretted canopy and three tall chimneys. A small separate building with a flat roof housed the gent's toilets; a small corrugated iron hut, described as a goods lock up, was later added after the opening of the extension through to Limpley Stoke in 1910. Otherwise the station facilities changed very little apart from modification to the track work to facilitate through working rather than terminal movements. A new signal box opened on 3rd May 1910 beyond and opposite the station. This replaced an earlier box west of the road bridge.

No major goods facilities were provided at the station; most local freight traffic was associated with the many local collieries. Following cessation of passenger services some deterioration of the station buildings set in but this accelerated after goods movements finished in 1951. By the following year the station roof was missing. Some readers will recall that in 1931 it was the location of filming for Arnold Ridley's 'The Ghost Train'.

Today in 2002 all traces of the former railway have gone and the actual alignment of the former line was not readily apparent to the author. Housing development has taken place to the west of the former road bridge which itself has also vanished.

CASTLE CARY

OPENED: 1st September 1856 (with the opening of the Frome - Yeovil section of the Wilts, Somerset & Weymouth Railway).

CLOSED: Passengers - remains open for services on the Bristol - Weymouth and Taunton - London lines. Goods - 3rd October 1966.

Castle Cary Station, over a mile north west of the town itself, opened originally with a passing loop on the single track broad gauge line from Westbury and Frome to Yeovil. The line was converted to standard gauge through the station in June 1874; the track was doubled from Witham to Castle Cary in 1880 and then on to Yeovil in 1881. Until 1905 services to, and from, Castle Cary were running on the line from Bristol and Westbury to Yeovil and Weymouth. With the opening of the new GWR cut off route to the west of England from Castle Cary to Cogland Junction north of Taunton in 1906, the station took on a new role as a junction. Trains from London to the west passed through, though few stopped at

Opposite top Camerton. A Cam Valley passenger train with staff and passengers posing for the photographer.

Bottom Castle Cary. The 'up' Cornish Riviera passing through in the early 1950s. The main buildings are on the up platform. Note the milk churns on the down.

Castle Cary; more significant was the introduction of a new stopping service from Westbury to Taunton.

The size of the station, and the facilities provided, evolved with the developing role of Castle Cary from 1856 to 1906. The original station buildings dating from 1856 were constructed of local stone and designed by one of Brunel's assistants, R.P. Brereton, the designer of many stations on the Wilts, Somerset & Weymouth Railway. The principal buildings were on the up (north) side of the track; when originally opened they varied little in size from the stone shelter on the down platform. However the up side building was extended in 1880, and, when the station took on its junction role in 1906, it was further extended eastwards providing a new waiting room and toilets; a canopy was also added. A cast iron gent's urinal and a corrugated parcels shed were erected on the up platform. A footbridge had been provided in 1897. The platforms were also lengthened by some 120 ft which overcame the former criticism that the platforms were too short and a safety risk.

In parallel with these developments of the buildings, changes were being made to the track layout and signalling. The old (May 1877) signal box at the Yeovil end of the down platform was too small to work the new junction and was replaced as from April 1905 by a brick built box, with typical hip gabled roof, nearer the junction.

The number of passenger tickets issued varied: 16,722 in 1903, 20,307 in 1913, 20,653 in 1923 and 17,012 in 1933. Staff levels increased from about seven in 1863 to thirteen in 1913 and nineteen in 1936.

Meanwhile Castle Cary's goods facilities were also developing, particularly during the years 1903 to 1907. Sited mainly on the up side close to the junction, these included a large brick goods shed (replacing an earlier shed behind the up side station building), a cattle dock and pens and a ten ton crane. Large amounts of coal were delivered by rail to the well known local firm of Snows who operated a coal delivery service from the goods yard, while the agricultural merchants Messrs Bibby & Co received and delivered agricultural feed to many local farms. Railway based lorries also operated a wide ranging

delivery service from the rail head to local farms and businesses. For some years a milk factory operated behind the station and milk was an important export to the London area.

The date of 3rd September 1942 was a fateful day for Castle Cary Station. At 9.14 that morning four bombs fell on and around the station, six people being killed and many injured. The signal box, goods shed and parcels office were damaged or destroyed though the main station buildings escaped major damage. A few days later normal working was resumed, the junction being worked by an emergency box brought from Reading, apparently one of a number kept for such emergencies. A new ARP style box opened on 27th October 1942, less than two months after the bombs fell. However the goods shed was not rebuilt until 1954/55.

After the War, services resumed at the 1930s levels but by the late 1950s decline had set in. A significant loss was the withdrawal on 10th September 1962 of the stopping services from Westbury to Taunton along the cut off line via Somerton. The Yeovil/Weymouth line was singled as from 12th May 1968 and the station closed to goods traffic on 3rd October 1966. The signal box closed on 3rd February 1985.

On a more positive note, in 1984 major attention was given to track-work and signalling and the opportunity was taken to re-build the down platform so that the Weymouth line trains could call at either face. This gave extra capacity at the station which was needed because of the welcome introduction of stopping West of England expresses en route to and from London. Castle Cary therefore now serves

Chard Central. A view from the north in about 1960. A Taunton bound train stands at the main through platform. The bay platform is to the right.

passengers making journeys to and from the capital as well as those travelling on the Bristol to Weymouth line. Some south Somerset residents travel regularly to work in London, a real up-turn in the fortunes of the station. A particular peak use of the station comes with the Glastonbury Festival held at nearby Pilton when music-lovers from all over the country use the station. Today the original main station building survives in good condition, albeit without the chimneys, but the 1856 down side shelter was lost in the rebuilding. The 1954/55 goods shed remains in commercial use - the former coal yard and sidings are now used as a car park, much needed with Castle Cary's developing role as a inter-city station. The former creamery building with chimney remains behind the station.

CHARD CENTRAL

OPENED: 11th September 1866 (with the opening of the Taunton - Chard Joint branch from the Bristol & Exeter Railway).

CLOSED: Passengers - 10th September 1962 (with the closure of the Taunton - Chard Junction line to passenger traffic).
Goods - 3rd February 1964 (private siding closed 3rd October 1966)
Temporary closure to all traffic 3rd February - 7th May 1951 due to a fuel crisis.

The station opened as Chard Joint, was renamed Chard on 1st March 1928 and renamed Chard Central on 26th September 1949. Even before the opening of the branch line from the south to Chard Town in 1863, the residents of Chard were determined to have a rail connection to Taunton. The branch was thus very much welcomed when it opened in mid 1866. Although built by the B & E Railway, the station was seen as a joint venture with the London & South Western Railway, with the opening of the spur line into the station from the south only two months after the Taunton line opened.

The station was a fine stone and brick building in Brunel style under an overall slate roof with vents. It was regarded by some as grandiose for a branch line with one through line (originally mixed gauge). Bay platforms were provided at both ends for use by trains from Taunton (north end) and Chard Junction (south end). The main building housed a booking office, waiting rooms, parcels office etc. For some years the GWR (which had amalgamated with the B & E in 1876) and the London & South Western Railway had their own station masters and booking offices. The southern bay platform was extremely long; built in three stages, it curved with the line. For some time it was covered by a canopy. Trains, however, ceased to use it from 10th October 1927. The northern bay platform, serving trains from Taunton until the station closed, remained in good condition with a distinctive GWR pattern water tower. The number of passenger tickets issued

Chard Junction. Looking up through the impressive covered footbridge.

remained fairly constant from 1903 to 1923: 25,901 and 24,782 but dropped greatly to 7,434 in 1933. Goods facilities, in addition to those provided to the south at the old Chard Town site, were to the west of the station, and included a goods shed and cattle pens.

The main station building, having previously served as a tyre depot, was occupied early in 2002 by Engine Parts (Chard) and Mark Chudley International Shipping. The appropriately named Great Western Car Sales and Old Station Court are nearby.

CHARD JUNCTION

OPENED: 19th July 1860 (with the opening of the Yeovil Junction - Exeter section of the London & South Western Railway).
CLOSED: Passengers - 7th March 1966
Goods - 18th April 1966

Opening in 1860 as Chard Road on the Yeovil to Exeter line, the station became a junction with the opening of the branch line to Chard Town on 8th May 1863. However, the station name did not change for another nine years until August 1872.

The main station buildings with the usual facilities stood on the up-side. A goods shed and cattle pens were on the north side of a siding that led into a bay platform on the up side at the Axminster end. The

Chard Junction. The isolated branch platform with canopy. The main station buildings are to the right on the Yeovil to Exeter line.

down platform housed a waiting shelter and gent's urinal. An early impressive wooden waiting shelter was subsequently replaced by a brick building. A covered footbridge connected the two platforms, though this was a later addition.

An unusual feature was that the branch line platform was physically separate on the up (north) side across the station forecourt. It was a simple bay platform with a canopy centrally supported on pillars though, from the mid 1950s, this was removed.

A dominating feature of the scene for many years, and still today, is the major milk depot behind the down platform into which sidings were laid in 1937.

Rail milk tanker traffic ceased from April 1980.

Following closure of the station in 1966 the up side buildings and goods shed survived into the 1980s and the latter is still in commercial use. Also visible are the up platform, traces of the main building floor, a signal box at the Crewkerne end of the up platform (the 1982 version replacing the 1875 original) retained to control the passing loop and the level crossing gates, remains of the branch platform (now in a coalyard), a small stretch of original fencing and a buffer within the expanded milk depot site. The adjacent Chard Road Hotel has been renamed the Three Counties Hotel, reflecting its location on the borders of Dorset, Devon and Somerset.

CHARD TOWN

OPENED: 8th May 1863 (with the opening of the Chard Road (later Junction) - Chard branch of the London & South Western Railway).
CLOSED: Passengers - 1st January 1917 (when the GWR undertook to work the line from Chard Junction to Chard Joint).
Goods - 18th April 1966.

Opened as the northern terminus of the branch from the Salisbury to Exeter line, this small station comprised a single platform upon which stood a one storey iron building (known locally as the 'tin shed') incorporating the usual offices. Beyond the building

Chard Town. The former passenger station in 1960, in use as a goods depot since 1917.

Charlton Mackrell. A local Taunton to Castle Cary train at the up platform on 10th April 1962.

was a shed and cattle pens. Opposite and west of the platform stood a large goods shed and associated sidings.

Following the opening of Chard Joint Station in September 1866 some half mile north of Chard Town as the terminus of the Taunton - Chard branch, a spur line was constructed from just short of the Town Station to link the two lines, opening on 26th November. However at this stage trains from Chard Junction proceeding through to Chard Joint still served the old Town terminus and had to back out before proceeding along the spur line. To overcome this problem, a platform with a shelter came into use on the spur line in 1871, adjacent to the Town terminus. There was a plan to close the original terminus but this did not come to fruition.

After gauge conversion brought easier movements in the Chard area and through trains ran from Taunton to Chard Junction, it was decided to close Chard Town terminus and the spur line platform at the end of 1916. The whole site took on a new role as the main goods depot for Chard. It continued to thrive into the 1950s but goods traffic ceased as from April 1966.

By 1967 the sidings had been lifted and today the old Chard Town site has vanished beneath road improvements and a new Tesco store. The spur line cutting has been filled in.

CHARLTON MACKRELL

OPENED: 1st July 1905 (with the opening of the Castle Cary - Charlton Mackrell section of the GWR cut off route Castle Cary to Cogland Junction).
CLOSED: Passengers and goods - 10th September 1962 (with withdrawal of local passenger services between Castle Cary and Taunton).

Charlton Mackrell opened as the temporary terminus (until 2nd July 1906) of the Castle Cary to Cogland Junction GWR cut off line. The station was of a standard form found on the cut off. The principal building with a horizontal canopy and incorporating the main facilities was on the up line platform; the down platform had a brick shelter and gent's toilets. A covered footbridge linked the platforms at the west end. Passenger numbers were relatively low and in 1913 5,638 tickets were issued, by 1933 this had fallen to 4,227. A goods yard with goods shed and cattle pens, a dock and a crane, was at the eastern end of the station site on the up side. A signal box was sited off the east end of the down platform. This closed on 3rd December 1963.

Today only Station Road remains, running under the railway at the west end. The up side station site and goods yard houses the Old Quarry, selling paving and building stones, whilst the site on the down side now contains the Charltons Community Centre with associated re-cycling facilities.

CHEDDAR

OPENED: 3rd August 1869 (with the opening of the Yatton - Cheddar section of the Cheddar Valley & Yatton Railway).

CLOSED: Passengers - 9th September 1963 (with the closure of the Yatton - Witham line to passenger traffic).

Goods - 29th November 1965. (Private siding facility withdrawn 28th March 1969).

The local tourist attraction of Cheddar Caves brought considerable numbers of passengers to the area and this, coupled with the town's trade in cheese and strawberries, justified a somewhat larger station than others on the line. It was in the typical B & E style with decorative barge boards, and for many years boasted an overall timber roof. Under this roof the booking hall and waiting room were provided on the north side facing out on to the main station approach road. A footbridge crossed the tracks under the roof and a refreshment room served customers for some years (closing on 29th September 1925). Passenger ticket sales declined markedly from 30,750 in 1903 to 8,139 in 1933 as visitors increasingly used cars or coaches.

A range of goods traffic was handled at Cheddar, a large goods shed being situated to the west of the station. Strawberries were particularly important in the summer months with passenger trains bringing pickers from the Bristol area and goods trains taking the fruit away.

Following closure to passengers in 1963, the roof was demolished a year later. Much however still remains. The station site is occupied by Wells Cathedral Stone Masons, with the main station building, complete with awning, surviving as part of the overall structure. The goods shed has been converted into a house, integrated into an adjoining housing development, whilst the station master's house, 'Station House', is also in residential use with gable barge boards intact.

CHILCOMPTON

OPENED: 20th July 1874 (with the opening of the Bath extension of the Somerset & Dorset Railway from Evercreech Junction to Bath).

CLOSED: Passengers - 7th March 1966 (with closure of the Bath Green Park - Poole line to passenger traffic).

Goods - 15th June 1964.

Sited to the west of the village on a double track section of the S & D, Chilcompton Station's main buildings were provided on the down (south) platform, including a general waiting room, ladies' waiting room, booking office and station master's office. A separate building contained the toilets. The buildings also faced onto the main station approach road which led from the B3139. A wooden shelter

Cheddar. From the west on 23rd June 1953. The overall timber roof is still in place. The main station building is on the left. (See also the photograph on the Contents page).

Chilcompton. A view from the south, with the main building with sloping canopy on the down platform (right) and wooden shelter with canopy on the up.

with canopy served passengers on the up platform. This was considerably longer than the down, which had a signal box at the west end. No footbridge was provided, only foot boards at the east end. As well as passenger traffic generated by the local community, the nearby Downside School was a source of much business. Special trains were sometimes run at the beginning and end of term and in some timetables the station appeared as 'Chilcompton for Downside'. A small goods yard with goods shed, cattle pens and a five ton hand crane was sited at the west end of the down side whilst a water column at the east end of the up platform was used by banker engines that had assisted heavy trains up the gradient from Bath. Chilcompton saw considerable movements of coal traffic with a siding a little to the west of the station on the down side serving a loading area for coal brought from the nearby New Rock Colliery.

After closure in 1966 the station site was used for storage by Sheppard's Saw Mills until it closed in the mid 1980s. Most of the station was cleared in 1991.

Today much of the site east of the station buildings has been redeveloped for housing with a new road, Station Mead, apparently on the line of the old station approach road. Beyond the new road, remnants of the former down platform can be seen in the undergrowth. Much of the railway land beyond the station is in use by Massey Wilcox, a local haulage firm.

CLAPTON ROAD HALT

Weston, Clevedon & Portishead Light Railway (*see p 150*)

CLEVEDON

OPENED: 28th July 1847 (with the opening of the Yatton - Clevedon branch of the Bristol & Exeter Railway).

CLOSED: Passengers - 3rd October 1966 (with closure of the Yatton - Clevedon branch).

Goods - 10th June 1963.

Clevedon opened in July 1847 as the terminus of the broad gauge branch from the B & E Railway at Yatton (prior to branch opening called Clevedon Road). The Yatton to Clevedon branch was worked by the GWR until the B & E Railway took over operation in 1849. This arrangement lasted until 1876 when the two companies amalgamated. On the 28th September 1879 the branch was converted from broad to standard gauge.

The 1847 station building comprised a wooden train shed together with associated timber offices. These facilities proved inadequate and in 1890 the whole station site was remodelled. The original goods shed was demolished thus allowing the platform to be lengthened; goods sidings were laid both east and west of the main branch line. The original broad gauge water tower remained.

A new larger building, constructed of local stone which harmonised with nearby buildings, was built, with the main facilities along the east side. The coal fire in the booking hall opposite the ticket window is well remembered A canopy over the main entrance was a feature of the station, an impressive structure for the terminus of a relatively small branch line. The original wooden train shed was left in situ and a stone curtain wall was erected to hide the view of

Clevedon. A general view of the station as remodelled in 1890. The original 1847 train shed covers the platform at the buffer end. Note the massive water tower.

Clevedon. The impressive 1890 station building including a canopy over the main entrance.

trains from the town centre. The train shed covered both the end of the main branch line and also a short spur off the run-round loop. Leading from the train shed a wide wooden canopy covered a further section of the platform, its width also providing cover outside the station itself in the adjoining yard. This long canopy was held in place by a number of fine ornamental brackets. Further south at the end of the relatively long platform was a timber signal box; this ceased working as from 1917 when the signalling system at Clevedon was simplified; from this time it only housed a ground frame adequate for working the terminus lines.

The new post 1890 arrangements provided Clevedon with two goods yards straddling either side of the passenger station. The new larger goods shed was to the west and, like the station itself, was built of local stone.

The branch opened with considerable hopes for its success as Clevedon was then the principal resort of the north Somerset coast. At the time the B & E Railway advertised Clevedon more than Weston-super-Mare (which was still in its infancy as a resort) and until 8th May 1879 there was a special 560 ft excursion platform at Clevedon. The situation did not last too long however and, by the beginning of the twentieth century, although excursion traffic still came, Clevedon had become established more as a dormitory town for Bristol and a centre for the retired.

In the early 1920s more than a dozen staff served the large numbers of passengers and a variety of freight. In addition to the commuting and day tripper traffic, school children were regular passengers either leaving Clevedon for schools in Bristol or coming to St Brandon's School in the town. Over the period 1924-1936 travellers from Bristol enjoyed the luxury of a through coach from Bristol, being slipped from a main line train at Yatton and then attached to a branch train. In 1951 61,070 tickets were sold at Clevedon. Goods traffic was varied and included cakes from the Hales factory in the town. Goods facilities were finally withdrawn as from 10th June 1963.

In its latter years the steam auto-trains used on the branch for many years were replaced by the early GWR diesel rail cars and then by standard DMUs. Clevedon became an unstaffed halt as from 20th April 1964, the Yatton station master taking charge of the whole branch. Complete closure came on 3rd October 1966; a total of 630 tickets were issued on the last day of services, the single car DMU being replaced by a two car unit.

The buildings at Clevedon were demolished in May 1968 and the whole site of the station and goods yard was subsequently redeveloped as the Triangle Centre by Tarmac Properties Southern Ltd. At the time the Company sponsored a leaflet on the branch line prepared by the author. Today the only reminder of the previous railway presence is a war memorial erected by Clevedon Town Council to commemorate the residents of Clevedon who left the town by the GWR to fight in the First and Second World Wars. There is a small section of railway line behind the memorial at the front of the shopping complex.

CLEVEDON

CLEVEDON ALL SAINTS HALT

CLEVEDON EAST HALT

Weston, Clevedon & Portishead Light Railway (*see p 150*)

CLUTTON

OPENED: 3rd September 1873 (with the opening of the Bristol & North Somerset Railway from Bristol to Radstock).

CLOSED: Passengers - 2nd November 1959 (with closure of the Bristol - Radstock - Frome line to passenger traffic).

Goods - 15th June 1964.

Sited in the valley below the main village, the station buildings were another example of the traditional William Clarke design on the Bristol & North Somerset Railway. The main structure, on the up line, incorporated the usual large horizontal canopy and three tall chimneys. Access to the station building was via a gateway alongside the southern end. A flat roofed annex at the north end housed the toilets, whilst a separate wooden building with a hipped roof was provided at a later date. The down platform, opened in September 1890, had a small waiting shelter complete with an angled canopy, again typical of the whole line. The platform also housed a signal box, used for the first time in 1890.

No footbridge was ever provided; inter platform movement was by footboards across the rails at the southern end. The station master's house was sited on the right of the entrance into the main station approach road on the village side

Passenger traffic was high at the start of the twentieth century with 24,468 tickets issued in 1903 but by 1933 this had fallen to 13,530. Children from the area going to independent schools in Bristol were regular passengers. For some years both passenger and goods traffic associated with the annual Clutton flower show were a part of station life, as were excursion trains to the south coast, Weston-super-Mare and Barry Island. Attractive flower beds featured at the station, as at many others in rural areas; in the case of Clutton they assisted with the frequent winning of the 'Best Station in the South West' award - due, it is said, to the station master's enthusiasm for gardening.

The station was important for many years for its goods traffic, especially in the main yard on the down side of the station which was approached by a separate entrance east of the railway bridge. In the 1920s and early 1930s the station and its yard were full of carts bringing in milk churns from nearby farms but by 1935/36 much of this was lost to road

Clutton. Looking south with the principal buildings on the up side (right), a fine example of the standard Bristol & North Somerset Railway design by William Clarke.

haulage. The yard included a small railway workshop. Timber for use there was a regular commodity as was coal for local business and domestic use.

Now there is little to be seen to remind one of this large station site. The main station buildings and platform have gone in an area of industrial development and in the lower goods yard, now a lorry depot, only one small building survives and a short length of track. The station master's house is still in residential use, with an extension on the east end, and a little up the hill into the village stands the Railway Inn.

COLE

OPENED: 3rd February 1862 (with the opening of the Templecombe - Cole section of the Dorset Central Railway).

CLOSED: Passengers - 7th March 1966 (with closure of the Bath Green Park - Poole line to passenger traffic).
Goods - 5th April 1965.

Cole opened in 1862 at the northern end of the Cole - Templecombe section of the Dorset Central Railway. On the same date, 3rd February, the Glastonbury - Cole section of the Somerset Central Railway also opened, thus completing a through route from Burnham-on-Sea to Templecombe. The Dorset Central and Somerset Central Railways

Cole. A Class 2P locomotive passes through the station heading south in July 1959.

amalgamated later in 1862 to form the S & D Railway.

The main stone built building was on the down platform; of typical Dorset Central design, it had high gables and tall chimneys but no canopy. On the up platform a small wooden shelter with an attractive valence was provided, this stood on an extension of the early short platform, at a slightly higher level. A separate gent's urinal was on the down platform adjacent to the main building; a further small stone building gave extra storage space. A small signal box stood immediately off the southern end of the up platform. The station master's house was behind the down platform; also adjacent was The Railway Hotel.

For many years life in Cole, now virtually a suburb of Bruton, has been dominated by schools - the Sunny Hill School of Girls, Sexeys School for Boys and Kings School, Bruton. These schools generated considerable traffic at Cole Station, as well as at Bruton on the GWR main line.

A small goods yard, behind the main building on the down side, included three sidings, a cattle dock, and, at one time, a small goods shed. It served local merchants and coal movements were particularly important. The goods facilities closed in April 1965 and the signal box just over a month later on 31st May. Passenger services lasted approximately a further nine months until March 1966.

The up platform shelter was demolished in June 1967 but, after remaining empty for some years, the station building was converted into a residence with a fine garden, 'The Old Station'. The station master's house remains in residential use, 'Station House'. During the 1990s further housing was developed on the former goods yard, the nearest house to the former station being called 'The Pines'. The former Railway Hotel is in residential use, 'Hillside'.

COLEHOUSE LANE HALT

Weston, Clevedon & Portishead Light Railway *(see p 150)*

COMBE HAY HALT

OPENED: 9th May 1910 (with the opening of the Camerton - Limpley Stoke line).
CLOSED: 21st September 1925 (with closure of the Hallatrow - Limpley Stoke line to passenger traffic). Temporary closure, originally as a war time measure 22nd March 1915 - 9th July 1923.

Opened with the line in 1910 this halt, in a cutting on the north side of the single track line, was constructed with a brick faced platform; a shelter and lighting (two lamps) and nameboard but no seating was provided. A long access footpath led down from a road, to the west of the site, that crossed over the 66 yd long Combe Hay tunnel. In the early days of the halt a complaint was made that this approach path was too narrow to allow passage of trolleys; this meant that heavy luggage and milk churns had to be manhandled down to the platform.

Today over 75 years after it closed to passenger traffic no trace of the halt can be seen.

COMBEROW

West Somerset Mineral Railway *(see page 157)*

CONGRESBURY

OPENED: 3rd August 1869 (with the opening of the Yatton - Cheddar section of the Cheddar Valley & Yatton Railway).
CLOSED: Passengers - 9th September 1963 (with closure of the Yatton - Witham line to passenger traffic).
Goods - 1st July 1964.

From its opening in 1869, until it became a junction point with the Wrington Vale Light Railway in 1901, Congresbury Station, to the west of the village and south of the A370, comprised only one platform on the eastern side of the Cheddar Valley line. On this platform stood an impressive Mendip stone building of standard B & E design with decorative roof tiles, cruciform ridge tiles and intricate barge boards which distinguished the original buildings on this line (eg Axbridge, Cheddar, Sandford and Banwell). An unusual feature was a short awning on the front of the building which sheltered the main entrance; this led into the general waiting room which in turn led to the booking office and ladies' waiting room/toilet. The booking office also served as the station master's office. Apart from a separate entrance into the gent's toilet/lamp room at the north end of the building, the waiting room door on the platform was the only entrance. Passengers gained access to the platform via iron gates adjacent to the north end of the building. There was no separate parcels office but extra storage was provided in a separate small building with attractive barge boards at the south end of the platform.

Linked with the construction of the Wrington Vale Light Railway, the station layout at Congresbury was re-modelled at the turn of the century. A long crossing loop together with a separate up platform was installed and brought into use on 14th April 1901; on this date a new signal box at the south end of the new up platform was also commissioned some eight months before the Light Railway actually opened. This replaced an earlier B & E box. No bay platforms were constructed as it was envisaged from the outset that the Wrington Vale trains would normally continue on to Yatton to connect with the main line trains to and from Bristol.

Combe Hay Halt. A distant view looking east in about 1930. The halt had closed some five years earlier.

Congresbury. Looking south towards Winscombe. Note the attractive B & E design station and goods shed. A camping coach stands between them.

On the new up platform was an attractive wooden waiting room with a chimney, a shallow bay window and half gabled roofing and also an open air cast iron gentlemen's urinal. No footbridge was ever provided, inter platform movements being via a foot crossing at the Yatton (north) end.

Passenger numbers were never great; the number of passenger tickets issued declined from 11,479 in 1903 to 3,477 in 1933.

From its opening, a goods shed, also of standard B & E design, stood south of the station on the down side; a line through the shed led to a loading bay behind the platform. For some years a camping coach was sited in the bay. In the 1930s a station master's house was built near the A370 on the village side of the line. The station master and his small staff for many years created excellent floral displays in the station gardens.

Today few traces can be seen of the station though the remains of two platforms are still in undergrowth on either side of the Cheddar Valley Railway Walk as it passes through on its route from Yatton to Axbridge. The former A370 road overbridge has been replaced by a level alignment north of the station site (Station Road); the former station master's house is still in residential use, as is 'Station Cottage', west of the former line. A new development, Station Close, is a further reminder of an earlier era.

COSSINGTON

OPENED: 21st July 1890 (with the opening of the Bridgwater Railway).

CLOSED: Passengers - 1st December 1952 (with closure of the Bridgwater line to passenger traffic).
Goods - 4th October 1954.

Sited just north of the village, the one platform stood on the south side of the single track line. Built of limestone, an impressive two storey station master's house adjoined the single storey station building which included a booking office, general waiting room, ladies' waiting room, station master's office, goods office and conveniences. For many years there was a canopy supported by four pillars over the platform itself, but this was removed after the Second World War.

A small loop line beyond the south west (Bridgwater) end of the platform led to a siding behind the platform. This served a carriage loading dock and five cattle pens, well used on Bridgwater market days.

The points at Cossington were operated from a ground frame hut sited on the platform close to the station master's house. This hut was a simple timber framed, weather boarded structure with a pitched roof and two six panel windows facing both up and down the track. It has now been transferred to the East Somerset Railway Centre at Cranmore.

Today the buildings are in residential use, the station master's house appropriately called 'Old Station House' and the station building, 'Station Cottage'. Three modern houses have been erected on the goods yard and a section of the track bed.

Cossington. The station building with canopy is dominated by the station master's two storey house.

Cranmore. Looking east towards Witham, the principal building and a gent's iron urinal on the up platform. Only a small wooden shelter on the down.

CRANMORE

OPENED: Passengers - 9th November 1858 (with the opening of the Witham - Shepton Mallet section of the East Somerset Railway).
Goods - February 1863.

CLOSED: Passengers - 9th September 1963 (with closure of the Witham - Yatton line to passenger traffic).
Goods - 17th January 1966 (except for a private siding).

REOPENED: 4th April 1980 (When trains commenced running to Merryfield Lane. The East Somerset Railway Centre had actually opened at Cranmore in 1975).

When the Witham to Shepton Mallet section of the East Somerset Railway opened in November 1858, Cranmore was the only intermediate station. It then comprised only one platform (later the up) on the original broad gauge track, though sidings were laid on either side. A loop line and the down platform came into use on 1st June 1880. Both platforms were extended and came into use on 2nd February 1912.

The principal building on the up platform, still in place today, is a limestone structure with a small canopy. It originally housed the booking and waiting facilities and the station master's office. A large house for the station master was erected behind the platform; this remains today in residential use. Gentlemen's toilets were originally provided in a separate timber clad building at the west end but this became rotten and was replaced by a standard GWR

cast iron urinal, which survives today. On the down platform stood a small wooden shelter with a chimney. A small signal box was originally sited beside the main building but this was replaced by a larger structure beyond the west end of the down platform; this closed as from 19th May 1963 and is now used for exhibitions.

Soon after the line closed to passengers in 1963 the down platform and shelter were demolished but the line remained open to serve a local bitumen depot, sidings to which ran behind the up platform. The station site was taken over by the East Somerset Railway with the backing of David Sheppard, the well known artist. A house was constructed to the east of the main building in 1974 and the East Somerset Railway Centre opened in 1975. The most significant project was the construction of a major new building in 1991, at the east end of the surviving platform, incorporating a spacious buffet, shop, art gallery and offices. Materials for its construction came largely from the former Lodge Hill Station (on the Cheddar Valley line west of Cheddar) and Wells Priory Road goods shed. The platform was extended to accommodate five coaches and a former bookstall from Salisbury Station was erected on the platform.

To the west of the station, sheds and workshops have been erected for restoration and maintenance of locomotives and rolling stock. The workshop came

from Devonport Dockyard and smoke vents from a former shed at Westbury. After a difficult period in the late 1990s, Cranmore Station is now the active centre of the East Somerset Railway which runs both steam and diesel trains at various times throughout the year.

CREECH ST MICHAEL HALT

OPENED: 13th August 1928 (on the Bridgwater - Taunton section of the Bristol & Exeter Railway originally opened through this site on 1st July 1842).

CLOSED: 5th October 1964.

Originally opened in 1928 at a cost of £600, it was extensively modified when the tracks between Cogland Junction, Taunton and Norton Fitzwarren were quadrupled in 1931. The two platforms facing onto the two relief lines had substantial shelters. Creech St Michael was one of a few halts on a four track main line and had facilities, including staffing, more akin to those of a full station. Access to, and links between, the two 300 ft platforms was via the adjacent road bridge. The floral displays were apparently subject to much praise and featured in the *Great Western Railway Magazine*. The platforms had tall posts on which pressurised oil lamps were raised by means of individual winches.

Today no remains have survived though changes in the brickwork on the adjacent bridge indicate the original gaps that gave access to the platform footpaths.

Creech St Michael Halt. Looking east towards Cogland Junction on 8th December 1963. As rebuilt in 1931, one of few halts on a four track main line.

CREWKERNE

OPENED: 19th July 1860 (with the opening of the Yeovil Junction - Exeter section of the London & South Western Railway).

CLOSED: Passengers - remains open for services on the London (Waterloo) - Exeter line.
Goods - 18th April 1966.

The station was sited over a mile south east of the town centre and close to the village of Misterton on the A356. It was, and indeed still is, a splendid example of the work of Sir William Tite, the architect who designed many of the stations on the London & South Western Railway. Further examples of his station designs on the Salisbury to Exeter line are Sherborne and Gillingham, both of which also still remain in good condition. The principal building, on the up platform (incorporating the date 1859), comprises two sections: the main offices under two hipped roofs parallel to the line, centred on a large booking office and a splendid three storey station master's house to the east. A long horizontal canopy completes the structure. Tite's designs were distinguishable by steeply pitched roofs and Crewkerne is a good example. On the down platform stood an impressive brick built waiting shelter with two small steeply pitched roofed sections at right angles to the track. An impressive covered footbridge linked the platforms at the Exeter end close to the A356 road bridge.

The goods yard with a large shed and a number of sidings was at the Yeovil end on the up side. It was

rather cramped on account of the relatively limited level site available; to assist shunting movements wagon turntables were in place for a number of years. It is recorded that, until the 1930s, some of the shunting movements in the yard were undertaken by a horse. The most northern of the sidings led into Bradford's coal yard. An original wooden signal box on the east end of the up platform was superseded on 6th November 1960 by a more modern, less attractive, version off the east end of the platform, which itself closed on 24th February 1967. The goods yard closed on 18th April 1966 and, associated with the unwise singling of much of the line in 1967, the down platform ceased to be used on 7th May. No passing place was provided at Crewkerne. The former up platform was lengthened in 1992.

A number of initiatives have been taken in recent years to improve the service on this southern route to the west of England and it now seems possible that double track will be restored on some sections. Crewkerne Station has seen extensive renovation work, particularly in the early 1990s, and today is one of the most impressive stations remaining in use in Somerset. Certain sections of the station have at times been let off to other users and, when visited in early 2002, the former station master's house was 'to let for office use'. The downside shelter has gone, as has the footbridge, though the two supporting legs of the latter remain in place. The 1960 signal box

Crewkerne. The fine William Tite design building on the up platform. The main station offices are beyond the dominating station master's three storey house.

Crewkerne. A 1999 view of the restored station building from the forecourt.

remains, though unused and derelict. Much of the former goods yard on the Crewkerne side of the station is used by Bradford Building Supplies. The former goods shed is used for vehicle maintenance. The old weigh-bridge house at the entrance to the station approach is also still in place, as is the weigh-bridge itself.

CROWCOMBE

OPENED: 31st March 1862 (with the opening of the West Somerset Railway from Norton Junction to Watchet).

CLOSED: Passengers - 4th January 1971 (with closure of the Norton Fitzwarren - Minehead line). Goods -6th July 1964.

REOPENED: 9th June 1979 (with the reopening of the Bishops Lydeard - Stogumber section of the restored West Somerset Railway).

The first sod on the West Somerset Railway was turned by Lady Isobel Acland Hood on 7th April 1859 at Crowcombe. Work then started in both directions undertaken by George Furness of London. The station, as originally built, comprised one platform on what is now the up (towards Taunton) side. On the platform was the station building and a stone built goods office which was demolished when goods traffic ceased. A goods shed was originally authorised but never built, all goods traffic being handled on a goods loading platform served by a long siding on the up side at the Minehead end of the station site. Cattle pens were sited behind the platform. A crossing loop, signal box and down platform with a wooden waiting shelter were added in 1879. Some ten years later on 1st December 1889, the station, which had opened as Crowcombe Heathfield, was renamed 'Crowcombe'. The 'Heathfield' was dropped to avoid confusion with the station at Heathfield in Devon.

These buildings continued in use throughout the

Crowcombe. An early view looking towards Taunton. The attractive stone building and small goods office stand on the up platform.

station's operations for the GWR and British Rail; the loop line and platform were extended at the Taunton end and came into use on 22nd April 1934. The 1879 signal box in the middle of the extended down platform was closed on 27th March 1966 and was subsequently demolished following a fire on 5th March 1967.

Following closure to goods traffic in 1964 and to passengers in 1971, the station remained unused until its reopening on the West Somerset Railway in June 1979 as 'Crowcombe', the suffix 'Heathfield' was added in 1991. One of the first developments was the replacement of the former wooden waiting shelter on the down platform which had been demolished by British Rail in 1967. Initially this was replaced by a former GWR bow ended hut which had served as a goods office at Flax Bourton. However, this was not considered very satisfactory and a new wooden waiting shelter was purchased and brought into use as from Easter Monday, 8th April 1996. The former Flax Bourton hut was transferred to a site above the up platform at the Bishops Lydeard end and following refurbishment, is now in use as a store.

For some fifteen years after reopening, only single line working was possible through Crowcombe but this changed from May 1994 when the crossing loop

Doniford Beach Halt. The re-erected GWR pagoda shelter in July 1998.

was reintroduced. At the same time a new signal box, which had been transferred from Ebbw Vale in South Wales some eight years earlier, came into use. In a typical 1930s GWR wooden top style, it houses equipment from a number of old boxes, in particular from Frome North Junction. Other features of the station in 2002 include a lamp hut on the up platform adjacent to the restored up side buildings, relocated from Meads Crossing at Huntsworth, and old style lamp posts, re-sited like those at Bishops Lydeard, from the former Tiverton Junction Station.

The base of the former goods office is to be seen under one of the platform seats. On the down platform is an exhibition of permanent way equipment and rails, including a section of Brunel's 7ft gauge track. Behind the platform adjacent to the new shelter is a greenhouse presented to the station towards the maintenance of the beautiful garden, currently a feature of this very attractive station. A new housing development alongside the former goods siding overlooks the line. The 1862 station master's house at the Minehead end, complete with traditional B & E barge boards, and now known as 'Puff Cottage', continues in residential use.

Donyatt Halt. A Chard Junction to Taunton train arrives at the halt on 8th September 1962.

DONIFORD BEACH HALT

OPENED: 27th June 1987 (on the Blue Anchor - Williton section of the reopened West Somerset Railway).

CLOSED: Remains open for passenger services on the West Somerset Railway.

A late addition to the Somerset's stations and halts, Doniford Beach, was opened by the West Somerset Railway in June 1987. It was built primarily to serve the nearby holiday complex on the former site of Doniford Army Camp. Standing on a curve with the west end under a brick built skew bridge that carries the coast road to Watchet, the platform is made of pre-cast concrete sections from the closed Montacute Station on the former Yeovil to Taunton line. A GWR corrugated iron pagoda shelter, obtained from Cove in Devon on the former Exe Valley line has been restored and erected on the platform.

DONYATT HALT

OPENED: 5th May 1928 (on the Taunton - Chard branch of the Bristol & Exeter Railway originally opened through this site in 1866).

CLOSED: 10th September 1962 (with the closure of the Taunton - Chard Junction line to passenger traffic). Temporary closure from 3rd February to 7th May 1951 due to a fuel crisis.

Some ¼ mile east of Donyatt village, this simple platform, faced with wooden sleepers and with a small wooden shelter, was sited on the east side of the single line in a small cutting. Access was via a path leading down from the road bridge at the Ilminster end of the platform; an ornate oil lamp stood at the top of the path; concrete posts with

brackets on the platform were provided to hang oil lamps in the winter, train guards having the task to light and extinguish them. A row of concrete tank traps lined the embankment behind the platform. These traps can still be seen in the undergrowth as can remnants of the wooden sleepers that faced the platform. By the bridge remains of a wooden gate indicate the original path entrance.

DRAYCOTT

OPENED: 5th April 1870 (with the opening of the Cheddar - Wells section of the Cheddar Valley & Yatton Railway).

CLOSED: Passengers - 9th September 1963 (with closure of the Yatton - Witham line to passenger traffic).
Goods - 9th March 1963.

Sited close to and south of Draycott village centre, the small station was on the northern side of a single line section of the Cheddar Valley line. The buildings comprised, from west to east: the station house, a small signal box, the main station building, a small metal shed, and a wooden store. Small flower beds completed the scene. The name Draycott Station dominated the station frontage. The small goods yard, which principally served local traders (particularly for strawberries) and the signal box were taken out of use on 9th March 1963; a wagon turntable in the goods yard had been removed much earlier in 1949. A large wheel in the signal box worked the level crossing gates to the west of the station; train crew apparently opened and shut the

Draycott. The main buildings. Note the prominent name and decorative barge boards, both of which are still present with its new residential use.

gates while the line remained open for limited goods traffic until 1969. Passenger ticket sales were never very high but declined from 9,720 in 1903 to 3,340 in 1933.

The station house and building on Station Road are now in residential use; the latter still boasts the name Draycott Station and the platform edge is also visible. The former station house still features the B & E barge boards and cruciform ridge tiles. A new house, named 'Level Crossing', stands adjacent to the site of the former gates.

DULVERTON

OPENED: 1st November 1873 (with the opening of the Wiviliscombe - Barnstaple section of the Devon and Somerset Railway).

CLOSED: Passengers - 3rd October 1966 (with closure of the Norton Fitzwarren - Barnstaple line).
Goods - 6th July 1964.

Dulverton Station was one of the original crossing places on the Barnstaple line when the Wiviliscombe - Barnstaple section opened in November 1873. It was actually sited some two miles south of Dulverton, south-east of the village of Brushford. This inconvenient location was overcome to some degree by a link bus service to the town which ran for some years. It was the most important intermediate station on the Barnstaple line with an extensive layout and a range of facilities that developed over the years. When the line opened in 1873 there were two platforms connected by a lattice covered footbridge with station buildings including a substantial station master's house and covered enclosed canopy on the up (north west) side; behind the Taunton end of the up platform was the goods yard and large goods shed. In 1902, when Dulverton Station became the northern terminus of the Exe valley line from Exeter, a bay was added to the down platform but in 1910 the platform became an island platform with the outer face serving a new loop line which usually served as the terminus of the Exe Valley trains. Extra sidings were also laid on the down side to supplement the original goods facilities behind the up. A small turntable was provided and also a large cattle dock. The original signal box was to the south-west of the station; this was replaced in 1908 with the arrival of the Exe Valley trains by a timber box on the up platform. This last was rebuilt in 1910 with a brick base.

Dulverton was, for many years, a busy station for freight. Goods traffic derived from the nearby Exbridge sawmills in addition to farm implements and agricultural produce. Whole cattle trains were assembled and set out from the station, and local hunting activities also generated movement of horses. This peaked with the annual Bampton Horse Fair. At the height of the station's prosperity some 20,000 tons of freight and over 23,000 passengers were handled annually, by a staff of fifteen. Soon after the Second World War staff numbers had reduced to nine. The northern part of the Exe Valley line closed on 7th October 1963 and freight traffic ceased on the Barnstaple branch on 6th July 1964. Much of the extensive track at the station was lifted, leaving only the two lines through the station. The signal box closed and only the up platform was regularly used until complete closure of the line on 3rd October 1966.

Following closure the station was taken over by the adjacent Caernarvon Arms Hotel sited on the Station Approach. This hotel had been built by Lord Caernarvon to serve visitors attracted to the area (travelling by train) for local fishing and to see the Exmoor scenery. The station site was grassed and levelled with the former station buildings used as staff accommodation for the hotel. The goods shed was adapted for hotel related uses.

Visiting in early 2002 the author found the whole site up for sale, including the hotel which had closed. The 'Station House and Plot' was to be auctioned separately. The site was advertised as having planning permission for 'residential use and a bistro'. The future of this once very busy railway scene was clearly in doubt.

Dulverton. Looking towards Taunton, the main buildings on the up platform including a large station master's house and single storey station offices with canopy.

Dunball. Looking north with the staggered platforms either side of the Kings Sedgemoor Drain.

DUNBALL

OPENED: 1873 (on the Bristol - Bridgwater section of the Bristol & Exeter Railway originally opened through this site in 1841).

CLOSED: Passengers - 5th October 1964.

Goods - 2nd November 1964.

At the point where the Bristol to Taunton and Exeter line emerges from a cutting at the western end of the Polden Hills and crosses the Kings Sedgemoor Drain, stood the small station of Dunball. The Drain itself

Dunkerton. The wooden building and signal box on the south side of the Cam Valley line.

resulted in the station platforms being staggered, the down platform north of the Drain and the up to the south. To the north of the up platform, sidings led west to a wharf on the River Parrett, crossing the main A38 road by a level crossing which often caused traffic delays. Wooden shelters stood on the two wooden platforms and a signal box was sited on the up side adjacent to the siding junction. On 6th November 1961, three years before its closure, staffing ceased and Dunball was re-designated a halt.

DUNKERTON

OPENED: 9th Mary 1910 (with the opening of the
Camerton - Limpley Stoke line).

CLOSED: Passengers - 21st September 1925 (with
closure of the Hallatrow - Limpley Stoke line to
passenger traffic).

Goods - 15th February 1951(with closure of the
Hallatrow - Limpley Stoke line).
Temporary closure to passengers 22nd March 1915
and to goods traffic 1st April 1918 as a war time
measure; reopened for passengers and goods
9th July 1923.

The station was a basic structure of a wooden
building with small canopy and two chimneys sited
on the platform south of the line. Facilities provided
in the building included a booking office, waiting
room, ladies' room with W.C. and a gentlemen's
toilet. A large corrugated hut at the west end of the
platform served as a goods lock up with a smaller
hut beyond the platform ramp being used as a store.
A signal box stood at the east end of the platform
controlling the loop line through the station. Cattle
pens were sited behind the platform and a small
water tank provided a water supply to the pens.

The station was located some distance from the
village, through which the main Radstock to Bath
road passed. The bus service provided strong
competition and, not surprisingly, passenger traffic
was low. In 1910 the staff comprised a station
master, two signalmen and two signalmen/porters.
This number gradually reduced first with the
temporary closure to passengers in 1915 and then to
goods in 1918. After reopening in 1923 no staff were
employed at Dunkerton, the station being the
responsibility of Camerton Station staff.

In early 2002 no trace could be found of remains
on the now derelict station site, apart from some
stone rubble that could have been part of the
platform. The access road was still there but securely
locked.

DUNKERTON COLLIERY HALT

OPENED: 9th October 1911 (on the Camerton to
Limpley Stoke line originally opened through this
site in 1910).

CLOSED: 21st September 1925 (with closure of the
Hallatrow - Limpley Stoke line to passenger traffic).
Temporary closure 22nd March 1915 - 9th July
1923, originally as a war time measure.

Initially it was not intended to provide a halt to serve

Dunkerton Colliery Halt. The GWR pagoda shelter
principally used by workers at the local colliery.

this locality but following representations from local
residents, the GWR agreed to provide a facility
principally to serve the colliery. The halt was also
intended to be for the benefit of the residents of both
Carlingcott and Tunley, although a stiff climb was
involved to both villages. Opening in October 1911,
a year after the line opened, the platform on the
south of the single track line was 150 ft long, 8 ft
wide and 3 ft high and surfaced with stone
chippings. The platform's front wall was more
substantially constructed than some other halts on
the Hallatrow - Limpley Stoke line, being built of
brick, and a corrugated GWR pagoda style shelter,
nameboard and oil lighting were provided. Access to
the platform was by means of a sloping path from
the adjacent road which crossed the line at this point
over an unusual shaped brick bridge. Total cost of
the halt was £230.

Today nothing remains of the halt, its site in a
cutting has been filled in. The unusual shaped bridge
is still there and two old railway lines, used as posts,
possibly mark the top of the original access path to
the platform south of the bridge.

DUNSTER

OPENED: 16th July 1874 (with the opening of the Minehead Railway from Minehead to Watchet).

CLOSED: Passengers - 4th January 1971 (with closure of the Norton Fitzwarren - Minehead line).
Goods - 6th July 1964 (with closure of the line to goods traffic).

REOPENED: 28th March 1976 (with the reopening of the Minehead - Blue Anchor section of the restored West Somerset Railway).

A single platform with a stone building, the station, originally costing some £900, stands on the down side of the line a mile north of Dunster village and castle. The building is of a similar design to the other two principal stations on the old Minehead Railway at Washford and Minehead. Dunster has windows similar to the former and a porch like that at the latter, though smaller. Its tall red brick chimneys are distinctive. The large canopy is also an attractive feature. The grand entrance to the small station reflects its past role as the arrival and departure point for distinguished visitors to the castle. Many of these played polo on the castle lawns, their grooms and ponies arriving in special trains.

The goods shed, also built in 1874, on a loop line at the east end of the station site, is on the up side.

Dunster. Looking west towards Minehead. The main station building is now well restored and used on the West Somerset Railway.

The loop was controlled until 1926 by a small signal box at the east end of the platform. The box was demolished when the platform was extended. The main goods inwards were coal and fertilisers, and outwards pit props and agricultural/horticultural products. A station master's house was provided at the east end of the site on the down side.

In 1934 with major growth in traffic to and from Minehead, the GWR decided to double the line from Dunster to the resort; a signal box was again required and a suitable box was brought from Maerdy in South Wales and erected at the west end of the platform. It continued in use until the line closed in 1971. When the West Somerset Railway reopened the line from Minehead, the Railway Inspectorate requested removal of the box from the west end of the platform to improve visibility at the level crossing. It was then removed as a whole on a specially adapted rail truck to Minehead where it is now the station signal box at the far end of the site beyond the long platform.

Since its reopening in 1976 much restoration has

Durston. Looking north on 16th February 1964 as a double headed special from Waterloo 'The Quantock Flyer' joins the main line from the Yeovil branch (top).

DURSTON

OPENED: Passengers - 1st October 1853 (with the opening of the Durston - Hendford (Yeovil) branch from the Bristol & Exeter Railway).

Goods - 26th October 1853 (with the opening of the Durston - Hendford branch to goods traffic).

CLOSED: Passengers - 5th October 1964.

Goods - 6th July 1964.

been undertaken at Dunster Station, now a listed building, and it is one of the most attractive on the reopened West Somerset Railway, serving visitors to the tourist attractions of Dunster village and castle. The annual 'Dunster by Candlelight' event every December brings a great influx of passengers, many on through excursion trains from well beyond Somerset. On occasion some 200-300 passengers throng the platform. The station's former parcels office is used by the Railway Printing Company which produces old Edmundson type tickets, on a machine brought from Crewe, for use on the West Somerset Railway and a number of other preserved railways. It was recently estimated that over six and a quarter million tickets had been printed at Dunster since 1990. A number of replica GWR lamps have recently been installed to add further to the station's amenities. The former goods shed, now a listed building, underwent major repair in 1992 and is now used by the permanent way gang of the West Somerset Railway.

Durston opened as a junction station in 1853 with the branch line from the Bristol to Exeter Railway to Hendford on the outskirts of Yeovil. There was relatively little local traffic but in its junction role, business was good. In 1933 24,490 passenger tickets were issued, a significant increase from the 14,588 in 1903. The main buildings and approach road were on the up side with a short siding leading to a small goods shed and cattle pens. The down platform was an island platform with a large signal box at the Bristol end opened in 1895; on the west side the platform served the down main line to Taunton and the east side principally served the branch line and stopping trains from Castle Cary and Westbury. In its early days this down island platform was narrower and a train shed covered the branch line. This was later removed and the platform widened.

An open footbridge connected the platforms at the Taunton end; this also spanned the branch line and descended to the road way outside the nearby Railway Hotel. Several goods sidings and a small turntable were also sited on the down side. These latter were taken out of use when the Yeovil branch closed in September 1964. The station itself closed a month later, for a short period it had only served stopping trains on the main line.

No significant remains of the station can now be traced, although the original Railway Hotel behind the down platform still stands. Railway cottages adjacent to the down side road approach also remain with the end house named 'Station House' and sporting a locomotive motif weather vane. Some original railings stand opposite the former Railway Hotel whilst the original up side goods yard is used for open storage behind locked gates at the entrance to the approach road. The site of the branch line junction north of the station is a large derelict area.

EBDON LANE HALT

Weston, Clevedon & Portishead Light Railway (*see p 150*)

EDINGTON JUNCTION

OPENED: July 1856 (on the Highbridge Wharf - Glastonbury section of the Somerset Central Railway originally opened through this site in 1854).

CLOSED: Passengers - 7th March 1966 (with closure of the Evercreech Junction - Highbridge line to passenger traffic).

Goods - 13th July 1964.

Opened as Edington Road, the station was originally named after the village of Edington some two miles to the south. This first station was a single platform on the south side of the Highbridge to Glastonbury line with no sidings. An increased role for the station came with the opening of the branch to Bridgwater on 21st July 1890, the name changing to Edington Junction. The old up platform became an island platform with the south side bay serving the branch line trains. A down platform with a wooden shelter was constructed on the now double track through the station. No footbridge was ever provided. The main wooden station building at the eastern end of the island platform incorporated a general waiting room, ladies' waiting room and booking office. A large canopy, providing shelter for the up and bay platforms, extended west from this main building.

A small goods yard with goods shed was located to the south of the station; cattle pens were provided. A timber framed signal box with a gabled roof stood at the west end of the island platform. There was a station master's house east of the station on the down side, adjacent to the level crossing on the north-south road from Burtle to Edington.

The station ceased to be a junction after complete closure of the Bridgwater branch in October 1954; passenger services had been withdrawn in 1952 and this led to the re-naming of the station as Edington Burtle from 8th June 1953. The down platform fell into disrepair and in February 1956 it was removed, along with the crossing loop and all sidings except

Edington Junction. Looking west in the 1930s at the island platform and canopy (left) and the down platform with wooden shelter.

that leading directly to the goods shed. The goods facilities were withdrawn altogether in July 1964 but the goods shed had gone. The signal box closed eight years earlier, in 1956.

Following complete closure of the station in 1966 some of the site, in particular the goods yard, was taken over by the National Rivers Authority, now the Environment Agency. The station house has been modernised and some of the trackbed through the former station has been incorporated into a garden in which a section of the former island platform is preserved. The former Railway Hotel, which stood north east of the station, has been re-named the Tom Mogg Inn after one of the station's last signalmen/porters. The Inn sign illustrates him holding the Somerset Central Railway hand bell rung at the level crossing in earlier times. One of the former level crossing gates is now in use at the Somerset & Dorset Railway Trust's site at Washford.

EVERCREECH JUNCTION

OPENED: 3rd February 1862 (with the opening of the Glastonbury - Cole section of the Somerset Central Railway).

CLOSED: Passengers - 7th March 1966 (with closure of the Evercreech Junction - Highbridge and Bath Green Park - Poole lines to passenger traffic).
Goods - 29th November 1965.

Nearly two miles south of Evercreech village, the station opened in 1862 with the new section of the Somerset Central Railway from Glastonbury to Evercreech Junction. A view north from the footbridge as an up train prepares to leave. Note the wide space between the platforms partly occupied by a short siding used by terminating trains and banker engines.

Cole. Initially called just Evercreech (Bradshaw listed it as 'Evercreech for Ditcheat'), the name changed to Evercreech Junction as from 20th July 1874 when the new Bath extension of the S & D opened northwards over the Mendips. (For a time the words 'for Castle Cary' were added). On the same date Evercreech Village (later New) Station opened on the new extension line adjacent to, and west of the village.

On the down platform (towards Templecombe) stood the principal station building with a canopy sloping down towards the line. This building was dwarfed by the station master's large house alongside. On the up platform stood a fair sized wooden shelter with a canopy sloping back from the line and a wooden hut providing storage for parcels and other goods. The distance between the platforms was relatively wide, resulting from the earlier broad gauge tracks through the site, and this space was occupied by a siding used by banking engines for trains over the Mendips and for storage of Highbridge line trains terminating at Evercreech Junction.

At the south east of the station was an open metal footbridge, connecting the two platforms, and a level crossing over the A371; beyond the crossing on the down side was a massive brick water tower topped by a metal tank. The signal box was on the up side

between the footbridge and level crossing, the latter being operated by a large wheel within the box.

The station's location at the heart of the S & D Railway's operations generated much freight traffic. Goods facilities at the station itself were focused in a yard behind the down platform accessed off the A371; the yard included a stone goods shed, a seven ton hand crane, loading dock and cattle pens. A further major complex of sidings was sited north west of the station on the up side and south of the actual junction. A further siding on the down side linked to the Somerset and Evercreech Junction Brick and Tile Works. It is not surprising that at peak times shunting activities at Evercreech lasted throughout twenty four hours! The handling of goods continued at Evercreech longer than at many Somerset stations but eventually ceased in November 1965. The station closed to passengers the following year.

Today the station buildings on the down side remain intact in residential use. The old station building is named 'Le Guichet' (French for booking office) and the station master's house, backing onto the former 'Goods Yard', is called 'Sdoog Dray'. The up platform buildings were demolished in February 1968 and a garage built on the platform itself. The track bed between the platforms has been filled in but the down side platform edge can still be seen. Industrial units have been developed on the former goods yards and also on a section of the track bed north of the station. The former Railway Hotel was at first re-named appropriately The Silent Whistle but is now called The Natterjack.

Evercreech New. Looking north towards Shepton Mallet with the main station building at the southern end of the down platform (right) and the tall signal box and wooden shelter on the up.

EVERCREECH NEW

OPENED: 20th July 1874 (with the opening of the Bath extension of the Somerset & Dorset Railway from Evercreech Junction to Bath).

CLOSED: Passengers - 7th March 1966 (with closure of the Bath Green Park - Poole line to passenger traffic).
Goods - 1st July 1964.

Conveniently sited on the western edge of the village, the station opened in July 1874 as Evercreech Village but was re-named Evercreech New two months later. The principal buildings, at the southern end of the down platform, included a station master's office, booking office, general waiting room, ladies' waiting room and a gent's urinal. A canopy, sloping towards the tracks, provided shelter. A cheese store stood at the north end. On the up platform was a small wooden shelter and tall signal box; a second box built in January 1920 replaced the first burnt down in October 1918. Access to the up platform was via wooden foot boards at the south end of the station.

Freight handling facilities were relatively small, only limited sidings being laid on either side of the double track line. A goods shed, with a travelling

Farrington Gurney Halt. The halt had one of the smallest shelters of any station or halt in Somerset.

crane, stood on the down side whilst the small up yard dealt with considerable milk traffic as well as lime from the Evercreech Limestone Company. Freight handling ceased on 1st July 1964 and the goods sidings, together with the signal box, closed on 11th October.

The station was demolished in 1968/69 and little trace now remains. The entire site, including the goods yard, has been developed for housing (Kiln Drive and Westbrook Road); a section of the station railings can still be seen forming a boundary fence to a parking area.

FARRINGTON GURNEY HALT

OPENED: 11th July 1927 (on the Bristol & North Somerset Railway originally opened through this site in 1873).

CLOSED: 2nd November 1959 (with closure of the Bristol - Radstock - Frome line to passenger traffic).

Located to the east of the village of Farrington Gurney, the halt, with its 150 ft long platform, was sited south of the single line in a cutting close to the point where the A362 crosses the Bristol to Radstock line. Provided in an attempt to counteract the competition of bus services operating on the A37, the halt's opening was marked by the running of a special excursion to Weston-super-Mare. The cost of the return fare was just two shillings (10p), so it was not surprising that over 300 adults and 140 children took advantage of the offer.

The halt was very basic with undoubtedly one of the smallest shelters of any halt in Somerset. As there was no booking office on the platform, tickets were issued through a window at the Miners Arms, a

public house some 40 yds to the west. Here a small room facing the halt was converted into a booking office, complete with ticket issuing box, dating press, train and fares books and a supply of leaflets and posters. The office was just behind the public bar but with no direct connection.

Today all traces of the halt and the line have gone. The cutting has been filled in, the bridge removed (though the southern parapet wall is still there) and the road re-aligned. The booking office window in the Miners Arms remains, clearly marked, over forty years after the halt's closure.

FLAX BOURTON

OPENED: First station - 1860 (as Bourton, on the Bristol - Taunton section of the Bristol - Exeter Railway originally opened through the site in 1841)
Second station - 2nd March 1893 (with the closure of the first station).

CLOSED: Passengers - 2nd December 1963.
Goods - 1st July 1964 (except for private siding to oil depot).

The first station, located in a major cutting west of Bristol, opened as Bourton in 1860. It was renamed Flax Bourton on 1st September 1888. The main wooden building on the broad gauge line was sited at the Bristol end of the up platform; a small shelter served the down platform. Access paths to the two platforms led down into the cutting from both north and south; these were linked by an unusual timber footbridge on brick pillars. A station master's house

Flax Bourton. The up platform of the first (1860) station with wooden building, signal box and unusual timber bridge with brick pillars.

Flax Bourton. The second station looking east towards Bristol. The site of the first station can be seen in the far distance by the high footbridge.

stood on the Bristol - Nailsea road close behind the up platform. With a need to expand facilities, a second station opened some 400 yards to the west on 2nd March 1893 and the first station closed. The main brick building with a large canopy was again on the up platform with a brick built shelter and canopy on the down platform. A covered footbridge, typical of the GWR in this era, linked the platforms at the west end. A siding on the west up side led to a dock and small goods shed with canopies on both the track and road sides.

Early in 2002 there were no remains of the first station; a section of the up side main building of the second station stood at the end of the approach road. Also in situ was the derelict goods shed with a canopy remaining on the road side. The approach road is now a private drive to new housing. The station house of the first station continues in residential use on the Bristol - Nailsea road - of interest is the typical B & E Railway decoration on the house gables.

FRESHFORD

OPENED: 2nd February 1857 (with the opening of the Bathampton - Bradford Junction branch of the Wilts, Somerset & Weymouth Railway).

CLOSED: Passengers - remains open for services on the Bristol - Westbury - Southampton/Weymouth line. Goods - 10th June 1963.

In the valley below the village itself, Freshford Station was built on a curved section of the single track broad gauge line. After the line was doubled in 1885, the main building was on the down side (towards Bath) with a waiting room and booking facilities and small canopy. Up side passengers were served by an attractive wooden shelter also with a small canopy. Inter platform connection was by an impressive covered footbridge at the north (Bath) end of the platforms. Flower beds were, for many years, a feature of Freshford, this being encouraged by the station master whose house was sited adjacent to the main station entrance, at the end of the steeply graded station approach road. Passenger numbers were relatively high for a rural station: in 1903 19,927 tickets were issued.

In 1910 sidings were constructed on both up and

Freshford. A view north towards Bath on 2nd June 1963. Note the large covered footbridge, unusual for a relatively small station, and the attractive gardens.

down sides of the line beyond the Bath end of the station. These were a part of the extensive loop line and exchange sidings system laid out in that year between Freshford and Limpley Stoke (Wiltshire) Stations with the opening of the Camerton to Limpley Stoke line through the Cam Valley. The sidings were well used by coal trucks from the Camerton line and its associated collieries. The 1910 signal box and the loop/sidings were taken out of use as from 18th August 1963, some two months after the handling of goods traffic ceased at Freshford Station.

Today, although the station remains open for passenger traffic (request stop only), the station is a shadow of its former self. Some sections of original gates and railings still remain but the flower beds are neglected. A basic 'bus shelter' provides cover on the down side, no shelter being provided on the up. The footbridge has been renovated but with no roof. The curvature of the line and the track cant (now increased on the curve for modern, faster trains) cause some problems to passengers who face a higher step than normal on to trains on the up platform. Early in 2002 it was reported on local radio and television that one resident found it necessary to have a box at the station to enable her to step onto, or alight from, trains at the up platform. The former station master's house remains in residential use as 'Old Station House'.

FROME

OPENED: 7th October 1850 (as the terminus of the Westbury (Wilts) - Frome section of the Wilts, Somerset & Weymouth Railway).
CLOSED: Passengers - remains open for services on the Bristol - Weymouth line.
Goods - 1967.

Frome Station was completed in the east of the town during the summer of 1850 in preparation for the arrival from Westbury of a further section of the Wilts, Somerset & Weymouth Railway. For some years it was a terminus before the next section to Yeovil opened on 1st September 1856; the line to Weymouth was completed in January 1857. These two extensions increased both passenger and freight traffic at this prime example of a Brunel design station.

The actual design is attributed to J.B. Hannaford, one of Brunel's assistants, the work being undertaken in the office of R.H. Brereton, Brunel's chief assistant. Frome Station is unusual in that virtually the whole building is constructed of wood whereas other stations with overall train sheds in the West Country were built of stone (eg Cheddar). The outstanding feature of Frome is the large overall roof constructed of timber rafters with slim wrought iron ties supported by wooden columns. Surmounting the roof is a full length glazed vent. Attached to the train shed on the up (town) side is a single storey building with a hipped roof, red brick chimney stacks and a

Frome. Looking north through the fine wooden roof which still survives. Note the canopy over the up and bay platforms at the far end of the shed.

small canopy. The principal station offices were within the single storey building including a booking hall and offices, waiting rooms (including, originally, separate first class and ladies waiting rooms), the station master's office, toilets and rooms for porters and for lamp storage. The booking hall led through to the up platform; on the down platform was another waiting room and for some years a typical GWR cast iron gent's urinal at the Yeovil end of the platform beyond the overall roof. On the up side was a short bay platform; this together with the end of the up platform itself was covered with an overall canopy. The platforms were linked after 1875 by a large covered footbridge immediately adjacent to the north end of the train shed between the shed and the bay platform canopy. Both platforms were extended, the up at the north end in 1893 and the down in late 1920/early 1921. A station master's house was built in 1882 close to the up side of the station.

Unlike some stations in Somerset, there was no local celebration to mark the opening in 1850. Some writers suggest that this was partly due to the local dismay at the length of time the line from Westbury had taken to reach Frome. Westbury had been linked to the rail system some two years earlier to the sound of local rejoicing. Although Frome residents were given a public holiday, no bands played, no flags flew and no church bells rang. A dinner was held at the Crown Hotel but only fifty attended, with some tickets unsold. The first train, an excursion to Oxford, left Frome Station at 7.0.a.m. on

7th October 1850 carrying about one hundred passengers. Four other trains ran to Chippenham and back. For the following 25 years, trains only ran through Frome on the line from Bristol and Westbury to Castle Cary, Yeovil and Weymouth. From 1875 a new passenger service began to Bristol via Radstock, these trains primarily using the bay platform. The opening of the Castle Cary to Cogland Junction GWR cut off route in 1906 brought a further increase in traffic through Frome which became a major bottleneck. This was relieved in 1933 with the opening of the Frome avoiding line east of the town.

In parallel with all these passenger services, Frome Station also developed for freight movements. A goods shed was built at an early date on the up side south of the station. Nearby were cattle pens, a cattle dock and a small wooden engine shed with a slate roof, opened in 1890. The principal goods facilities built on this side were close to the main station offices. As with many stations, sidings were also laid to adjacent factories, in this case serving the large malting building of E. Bailey (opened 1891, closed 1967) that dominated the station yard; a further siding served the major creamery also adjacent to the station approach. On the down side a long goods loop ran behind the station buildings; this linked to a smaller goods yard that incorporated a six ton capacity crane.

All these passenger services and freight movements meant that staffing levels were relatively high for a country town station; the staff averaged forty to fifty between 1900 and the Second World War. This had risen from five in 1850, eight in 1872 and thirty one in 1881.

Glastonbury and Street. The impressive 1870s station in difficult operating conditions.

Decline set in from 31st December 1959 when the last passenger train left Frome for Bristol via the Radstock line. The engine shed closed in September 1963 and, most significantly, the track was singled through the station on 19th August 1970. The up bay platform was taken out of use as from 17th May 1971. The footbridge was no longer needed and was removed. By the early 1970s, the whole station structure was in a bad condition and the train shed needed to be propped up with a steel post. With large costs likely for renovation, British Rail proposed complete demolition with replacement of the train shed by a bus shelter structure. Public outcry led to the station being listed as a Grade II Building of Architectural and Historic Interest. A number of major renovation initiatives have been undertaken and today the station has the last surviving example of an overall Brunel type wooden roof. Much of the area surrounding the station has been redeveloped - the creamery has closed, the site being used by a builders' merchants (Jewsons), and the malting building demolished except for a section of the rear wall. The site of the engine shed and much of the goods yard including the goods shed is now also used by Jewsons. The station master's house remains in residential use while the nearby former Railway Hotel has been renamed, 'The First and Last'.

GLASTONBURY AND STREET

OPENED: 28th August 1854 (as the terminus of the Highbridge Wharf - Glastonbury section of the Somerset Central Railway).

CLOSED: Passengers and goods - 7th March 1966 (with closure of the Evercreech Junction to Highbridge line).

Glastonbury opened as a terminus with the completion of the Highbridge Wharf to Glastonbury section of the Somerset Central Railway. The branch line to Wells opened on 15th March 1859 and the eastwards extension of the Somerset Central Railway to Cole opened on 3rd February 1862. The suffix 'and Street' was added in July 1886.

The station developed from a small building into an imposing structure with mostly wooden buildings dating from about 1878. The down (north) platform was an island some 290 ft long covered for half its length by a large canopy, the northern face being used mainly by Wells branch line trains until closure of the branch on 29th October 1951. From 1899 until 1932 the island platform building was largely occupied by refreshment rooms. The principal station offices, including a general and a ladies' waiting room, a booking hall and office and the station master's office, were sited on the up (south) platform which was also covered by a canopy. For

Hallatrow. Looking south towards Radstock on 16th June 1963. An impressive footbridge connects the two platforms, the principal buildings being on the down platform (left).

some years there was also a W. H. Smith bookstall on this platform. A siding immediately behind the up platform led to a loading dock. The two platforms were connected by an impressive lattice glazed covered footbridge at the east (Wells) end; this remained intact until the station's closure. Water columns were provided on both platforms.

A large timber signal box stood at the west end of the up platform controlling movements at the station itself, in the goods yard and around the station approaches. The goods yard, sited on the up side behind the station, was extensive with two hand cranes and eight sidings, serving a goods shed, cattle pens, loading dock, a saw mill and coal wharves. The yard saw much traffic during its life, including footwear from the nearby Clarks factories at Street. During the Second World War the yard area was used as a United States army transit camp.

The original offices of the Somerset Central Railway were located in a large red brick building now known as 'The Pollards', near the entrance to the station approach south east of the station. Constructed in 1861 as the Abbey Arms and Railway Hotel, part of it was leased to the Somerset Central Railway (and subsequently the S & D) who used it as their headquarters until this role was transferred to Bath in 1877. The building is still in situ used as administrative offices for the nearby Snow's timber yard.

The station remained largely intact for some years after its closure in 1966; it was eventually dismantled in 1984. Transferred to St John's car park, the island canopy took on a new purpose in providing shelter for Glastonbury's covered market. The remainder of the main station site was cleared in the mid 1980s. Today level crossing gates stand where the original line from Wells, now used as a road, entered the station site from the north east. Buildings in a former civil engineers' yard, north of the station, are now used for a variety of industrial uses and residential, 'Railway Cottages'.

HALLATROW

OPENED: 3rd September 1873 (with the opening of the Bristol & North Somerset Railway from Bristol to Radstock).

CLOSED: Passengers - 2nd November 1959 (with closure of the Bristol - Radstock - Frome line to passenger traffic).
Goods - 15th June 1964.

Serving the villages of Hallatrow and High Littleton, the station was initially opened with a single platform on the down side of the single track line. Constructed of local stone to the standard William Clarke design used on the Bristol and North Somerset line (including a large horizontal canopy with fretted edges and three tall chimneys), the main station building provided the usual facilities found in a rural station of this size. Entrance to the platform from the approach road was by a gate at the southern end of the building. Doors were not provided in the forecourt elevation of the design and double doors on the platform side led into the waiting room and booking office. The ladies' waiting room was accessed through another door from the platform whilst a third door in the building front led to a store.

With the extension of the Hallatrow to Camerton branch through to Limpley Stoke work commenced

66

on expanding the station facilities, in particular providing a new up platform (400 ft long) and extending the existing down platform (to 452 ft) The latter was in a slightly staggered position to the south of the up platform. Passengers on the up side were provided with a red brick waiting shelter with slate roof, chimney and small canopy. The new platforms were connected by an impressive footbridge with pitched roof to cover both the bridge itself and the steps which connected to the platforms in opposite directions - the down to the north and the up in a southerly direction. A new signal box was erected beyond the north end of the up platform and finally in 1912 a wooden parcels office was provided on the down platform at a cost of £55. In summary Hallatrow, with these developments around 1910, became a significant rural junction station. The total cost of the enlargements, including engineering and signalling works was £8,790.

In addition to passenger traffic Hallatrow was also a major centre for freight traffic. A goods shed and cattle pens were located in a goods yard north of the station on the down side. Goods handled, in addition to the usual local trade for Hallatrow itself and surrounding villages, included items from three local shoe and boot factories and books and magazines from Purnell's factory at Paulton. Hallatrow was also the nearest station to Farrington Gurney where, during the 1920s and 1930s, a very popular market was held. The local halt did not handle freight and all livestock movements were dealt with at Hallatrow. However, milk was by far the greatest source of goods traffic at Hallatrow with over thirty farms in the area sending all their output by rail first to Bristol and then on to London and South Wales. With milk brought to the station in churns, receipts were apparently some £300 per month during the late 1920s but in 1931 Express Dairies started a collection by road and the farmers deserted the railway entirely.

Both passenger and freight traffic continued at a reasonable level during and after the Second World War, the former despite strong competition from buses on the A37 route into Bristol. Closure of Hallatrow Station to passengers came in 1959 and to freight in 1964. All traffic on the line finally ceased in 1968, triggered by the great July storm which did so much damage in the north Somerset area.

Today a number of significant features of the station can still be seen. The main station building, complete with a section of canopy is now incorporated in a large house, 'The Ticket Office',

Ham Green Halt. The unusual provision of two GWR pagoda huts principally serving passengers visiting the nearby isolation hospital.

with an extension built on the former trackbed. The former goods yard is now used as a major storage area - J.A. Pitt European Warehousing and Distribution. Stretches of the former platforms can be seen leading south towards the road bridge and a former GWR notice stands on the side of the long north-south approach road. South of the road bridge the former station master's house remains in residential use close to the former bridge parapets and the Old Railway Inn, with a railway carriage in the garden housing restaurant facilities, is another reminder of an important rural junction station.

HAM GREEN HALT

OPENED: 23rd December 1926 (on the Portishead branch originally opened through this site in 1867).

CLOSED: 7th September 1964 (with closure of the Portishead branch to passenger traffic).

Built to serve both the residents of Ham Green village and visitors to the nearby Ham Green Hospital, the halt was opened during the campaign by the GWR in the 1920s to attract more passenger traffic to the Portishead branch. Largely constructed of timber, the single platform was unusual in being provided with two GWR pagoda hut shelters, reflecting demands at peak visiting times to the hospital. Although closed for nearly 40 years, part of the old platform can still be seen on, and adjacent to, the Ham Green viaduct over which the new freight services to Royal Portbury Dock now run.

HAM LANE HALT

Weston, Clevedon & Portishead Light Railway (*see p 150*)

HAMPTON ROW HALT

OPENED: 18th March 1907 (on the Bath - Wootton Bassett section of the GWR Bristol - London line originally opened through this site in 1841).

CLOSED: 29th April 1917.

A small halt with up and down platforms on the eastern edge of Bath, it was only open for ten years. No trace of the halt can now be seen and no photographs are known to exist.

HATCH

OPENED: 11th September 1866 (with the opening of the Taunton - Chard Joint branch from the Bristol & Exeter Railway).

CLOSED: Passengers - 10th September 1962 (with closure of the Taunton - Chard Junction line to passenger traffic).

Goods - 6th July 1964.

Temporary closure to all traffic from 3rd February to 7th May 1951 due to a fuel crisis.

Located in a cutting south of Hatch tunnel, the platform and buildings of a classic Brunel style were on the west side of the single track branch line. The mellow brickwork, arched windows, two tall chimneys and ornate lamps provided attractive facilities. A large goods shed stood just south of the platform and a cattle pen was sited in front of the shed, later converted into a loading ramp. A signal box built in 1892 closed after 64 years on 23rd September 1956. A goods loop provided a further facility opposite the platform; this was also taken out of use in September 1956. The station name-board with cast iron letters dated from the early B & E days. The number of passenger tickets issued peaked at 10,340 in 1923; this had fallen to 3,952 a decade later.

The main station building and goods shed remain in situ in industrial and storage use at the heart of an industrial development (Sterling Services, a stone/masonry firm). Original fencing with a kissing gate also remains along the west side boundary with the adjacent road.

HENSTRIDGE

OPENED: 10th September 1863 (with the opening of the Blandford St Mary - Blandford - Templecombe section of the Somerset & Dorset Railway).

CLOSED: 7th March 1966 (with closure of the Bath Green Park - Poole line to passenger traffic).

Goods - 5th April 1965.

North-east of Henstridge village, on the west side of a single track section of the S & D line, the station

Hatch. The Brunel style building on the west side of the track. The large goods shed is seen beyond the building both of which still exist in industrial/storage use.

Henstridge. Looking north towards Templecombe, the main wooden building at the smallest station on the S & D line from Poole to Bath.

opened in September 1863. It was the smallest station on the S & D's main line from Poole to Bath; there was no passing loop and the platform was only 150 ft long. The main building was constructed of wood with a slate roof and two chimneys. Facilities included a general waiting room, a ladies' waiting room with toilets, a separate gent's urinal and a booking office. A separate iron building provided extra storage. Passenger traffic was light throughout the station's life.

A goods yard, on the up side to the north, incorporated a loading gauge, cattle pens, a one ton

hand crane and a milk dock. Goods traffic at Henstridge ceased in 1965.

A station agent's house was sited behind the station alongside a small level crossing with Blackmoor Lane; the title 'station agent' was often used by the S & D, rather than station master. The station building itself, and part of the platform, was demolished in 1968. In the mid 1990s the remaining section of the platform was demolished and the site to the west of the station was redeveloped for housing, with one of the houses called 'The Sidings'. Today a gravel pedestrian path is laid along the previous rail alignment. At its southern end all four posts of the original Blackmoor Lane level crossing are still in place, as is one of the former gates. Remnants of the other gate lie beside one of the posts. The former station agent's house continues in residential use.

Highbridge (GWR). An early view north showing the wooden platforms, the tall chimneys on the up side building and the original covered footbridge.

HIGHBRIDGE (GWR)

OPENED: 14th June 1841 (with the opening of the Bristol - Bridgwater section of the Bristol & Exeter Railway).

CLOSED: Passengers - remains open for services on the Bristol - Taunton - Exeter line.
Goods - 2nd November 1964.

Highbridge was one of the original stations when the first section of the broad gauge B & E line opened from Bristol to Bridgwater in June 1841. When the Somerset Central opened its line from Highbridge Wharf to Glastonbury in 1854 it crossed the B & E line on the level just north of the station under a road

Highbridge (S & D). Looking east towards the distant Highbridge works of the S & D (top right). A train stands in the terminal bay.

bridge (B3139). Substantial buildings were provided on both up and down platforms in a typical early B & E Brunel style with horizontal canopies. The principal building on the up side, to which the station access road led, was originally surmounted by tall chimneys. A large covered footbridge provided a link between the platforms, though this was later replaced by a concrete structure which also linked to the adjacent S & D station to the east. To the north of the station on the up side were goods facilities including a large goods shed. For many years a large signal box stood between the footbridge and the road bridge at the north end of the down platform to work the many tracks on both the main and S & D lines. This closed on 20th March 1972 and was subsequently demolished.

Through the years the station name changed a number of times, particularly in later years. Opened as Highbridge, it was renamed Highbridge West on 5th May 1950, Highbridge and Burnham-on-Sea on 30th June 1962, Highbridge on 6th May 1974 and finally Highbridge and Burnham on 17th May 1991.

In early 2002 little remains of the old station apart from gates and railings, the main buildings having been demolished in the 1970s. The former goods yard and shed north of the road have gone.

The station remains open, served by local trains on the Bristol to Taunton and Exeter line. Small shelters are provided on both platforms, a brick structure on the down side and a 'bus' shelter and another small shelter on the up. The concrete footbridge continues to link the two platforms, though truncated at the east end where it originally also led to the now vanished S & D station. There is a well tended flower bed on the down side. In the 1990s the station approach area was improved with a new car park and a small public park with seats.

HIGHBRIDGE (S & D)

OPENED: 28th August 1854 (with the opening of the Highbridge Wharf - Glastonbury section of the Somerset Central Railway).

CLOSED: Passengers - 7th March 1966 (with closure of the Evercreech Junction - Highbridge line to passenger traffic).
Goods - 2nd November 1964.

The second to open at Highbridge, this station served traffic on the Somerset Central line opened in 1854 from the Wharf at Highbridge across the Somerset Levels to Glastonbury. Its name changed to Highbridge East on 26th September 1949. Surprisingly, the station had a total of five platform faces; these served two terminus tracks and also two through tracks which, after converging west of the station, crossed the GWR main line on the level. The station was immediately adjacent to, and east of, the

B & E (subsequently the GWR) station. The main building was of brick with stone facings and in its early days had a small canopy. Incorporating a booking office, station master's office, a general waiting room and a ladies' waiting room, it was sited at the buffer stop end of the terminal platforms. A bronze war memorial, formerly sited in the S & D locomotive works was set in its western end commemorating those who, in the employ of the S & D, gave their lives in the First World War. Two platforms, up (towards Burnham-on-Sea) and down (towards Glastonbury), principally served passengers on the through line to Burnham-on-Sea, following the opening of this extension in 1858. The only facility provided on these through platforms was a wooden waiting shelter with a small awning on the up platform at its western end. This platform was extended eastwards in 1932 with concrete components including fence panels.

The platforms of the S & D station were first linked by an iron footbridge with wooden approach panels in 1896. This also linked to the footbridge over the adjoining GWR station. This original bridge was replaced in 1933 by a concrete structure, a shortened section of which still connects the two platforms of the surviving station on the Bristol - Taunton line. In its early days tracks in the S & D station area were served by small signal boxes but later control over all the track work in the area of the two stations was taken over by a large signal box at the north end of the GWR station. One of the former small boxes, Highbridge A, stood adjacent to the footbridge steps and, following closure, operated as a staff mess room for many years.

Some goods traffic was handled in a small yard to the north of the station but the main S & D goods yard, including a large goods shed, was west of the main line crossing towards Highbridge Wharf. The principal activity that brought freight and passengers to the station itself was the Highbridge Works of the S & D Railway, opened in 1862, about half a mile east of the station. This was the headquarters for the repair of locomotives and rolling stock for the Railway and an extensive site provided a large range of facilities. The need for economy led the S & D to close the works in 1930, leading to 300 redundancies, a bad blow for the economy of Highbridge.

Following closure to goods in 1964 and passengers in 1966, the station was demolished in December 1970. Up until the mid 1980s, the former up concrete platform could still be seen but this has

Ilminster. The attractive station with arched windows and doorways. Today the building remains in excellent condition on an industrial estate.

been buried under the rubble and top soil which now covers the entire station site. Apart from the truncated concrete footbridge from the GWR station, no trace of the S & D station remains. The former goods yard west of the main line has been redeveloped for housing and a car park.

ILMINSTER

OPENED: 11th September 1866 (with the opening of the Taunton - Chard Joint branch from the Bristol & Exeter Railway).
CLOSED: Passengers - 10th September 1962 (with closure of the Taunton - Chard Junction line to passenger traffic).
Goods - 6th July 1964.
Temporary closure to all traffic from 3rd February 1951 to 7th May 1951 due to a fuel crisis.

Sited west of the town, Ilminster Station was a single storey building standing on the east side of the single track (originally broad gauge) branch line. The adjacent cattle market opened soon after the station. It was an attractive brick built structure with arched windows and a low pitched roof with elegant chimneys at either end. A central booking hall gave access from the station forecourt to the platform. An iron shed on the platform was for goods conveyed by passenger trains.

A signal box stood opposite the platform and a loop line enabled goods trains to cross passenger trains. A large brick built goods shed and cattle dock stood south of the platform and buildings.

At one time Ilminster station was staffed by a station master, general clerk, signalman, porter/signalman, two delivery drivers and a porter. In 1913 31,541 passenger tickets were issued but by 1933 this number had fallen to 6,897.

The station building is now in an industrial estate, in excellent condition, and occupied by an interior design firm. The goods shed, also well maintained, is in use as a carpet showroom.

ILTON HALT

OPENED: 26th May 1928 (on the Taunton - Chard Junction line originally opened through this site in 1866).

CLOSED: 10th September 1962 (with closure of the Taunton - Chard Junction line to passenger traffic). Temporary closure from 3rd February to 7th May 1951 due to a fuel crisis.

This was a basic halt on an embankment a little to the north of Ilminster; a seat was provided but there was no shelter. At either end of the platform was a stanchion from which oil lamps could be hung to light the halt. A pillbox at the north end of the platform was part of a north/south wartime defence line from the River Parrett to the south coast. Access to the halt was via a narrow path, apparently muddy in winter. A wooden structure on the right hand side of the path could have provided shelter for passengers. Early in 2002 there was no trace of the halt; the pillbox remained, though very overgrown. The approach path was muddy!

Ilton Halt. The basic halt on 5th September 1960. A seat was provided but no shelter.

KEINTON MANDEVILLE

OPENED: 1st July 1905 (with the opening to passengers and goods of the Castle Cary - Charlton Mackrell section of the GWR cut off route Castle Cary to Cogland Junction).

CLOSED: Passengers and goods - 10th September 1962 (with withdrawal of local passenger service between Castle Cary and Taunton).

The station, sited to the east of the A37 and a mile south east of the village, was one of three stations and halts that opened in July 1905 on the first section of the GWR cut-off route. The other two were Alford Halt and Charlton Mackrell. Keinton Mandeville Station was almost identical to the one at Charlton Mackrell.

The main building, incorporating the principal offices, with a horizontal canopy, was on the up line. A brick built shelter with a small canopy stood on the down platform and a covered footbridge linked the two platforms at the west end. Passenger numbers were slightly less than at Charlton Mackrell: in 1913 4,681 passenger tickets were issued. A small goods yard was provided on the up side to the north east of the station including cattle pens, loading dock, a crane and small goods shed. A signal box, opened with the line, was sited beyond the east end of the down platform; this continued in use until 22nd September 1964, two years after passenger and goods traffic ceased at the station.

The station site and goods yard is now principally occupied by a scrap-yard for cars, Cross Keys Motor Services. Small sections of the building and platform on the down side survive.

KELSTON

OPENED: 1st December 1869 (on the Mangotsfield (Glos) - Bath branch from the Bristol - Gloucester line, originally opened through this site four months earlier).

CLOSED: 1st January 1949.

Kelston opened in December 1869 with only three trains stopping each way daily and none on Sundays. For a few months after its opening it was called Saltford. Later the timetable referred to Kelston for Saltford. Although the original earthworks allowed space for sidings to be laid, this option was never implemented. The basic stone-built offices were on the down (north) platform, only a timber shelter being provided on the up. The station was three quarters of a mile from Kelston, reached by a footpath across the fields, and was much closer to

Keinton Mandeville. Looking west towards Taunton. The principal building is on the up platform. Note the milk churns on the down.

Saltford just on the other side of the River Avon. A footpath parallel to, and north of, the line led from the station over the river bridge and down a slope to the lower parts of Saltford.

The station was particularly busy on the day of the annual Saltford Regatta and also when race meetings were held at Bath race course, some two and a half miles away, and 700 ft uphill. Race trains ceased to

Kelston. Looking towards Bath. The main building on the down side (left), only a wooden shelter on the up.

use the station after about 1930. Many of the passengers using Kelston Station were anglers out for a day's fishing in the River Avon. With ever reducing passenger numbers, the last train to stop was the 7.05 p.m. from Bristol on 31st December 1948 after which the station's sole employee retired. The building on the down platform was not demolished until 1954.

Today, nearly 50 years on, no significant remains of the station can be seen on what is now the Bristol - Bath cycle way. Raised banks either side of the cycle-way indicate the site of the old platforms and stone rubble could derive from the old station buildings. The footpath to the River Avon bridge remains with iron railings alongside.

KEYNSHAM

OPENED: 31st August 1840 (with the opening of the Bristol Temple Meads - Bath Spa section of the GWR Bristol - London line).

CLOSED: Passengers - remains open for services on the Bristol Temple Meads - Bath line.

Goods - 29th November 1965 (except for a private siding).

Keynsham was the only intermediate station when the GWR line opened for passengers in August 1840. The first train from Bristol reached Keynsham in fourteen minutes, stopped for three minutes for passengers to alight and get on, and then proceeded on to Bath. The first train to arrive in Keynsham from Bath was forty three minutes late due to 'operational difficulties in the Bath area'! Records indicate that, on the opening day, takings amounted to £21 14 0. The fares from Bristol to Keynsham were 1st Class 1/6 (7½p) and 2nd Class 9d (4p). No third class carriages were provided by the GWR at this time. There were no return fares. In the 1840 timetable there were ten trains a day between Bristol and Bath, with six calling at Keynsham.

In his official 1861 *Guide to the Great Western Railway*, George Measom described the original two storey Tudor style building on the up platform as 'constructed of hammer dressed lias with Bath stone quoins and dressings'. The main entrance to the station was beside the building, which included accommodation for the station master on the upper floor. The building originally contained a mosaic pavement from a Roman villa, discovered when a cutting was made on the line near Newton St Loe, but this was removed to the Bristol City Museum in 1851.

On the down platform a shelter served passengers travelling to Bristol. The overall scale of the station buildings could be considered out of proportion for the size of Keynsham, with only some two thousand inhabitants at that time. In 1884 the GWR directors authorised further expenditure for widening the down platform, the provision of a new waiting room and a footbridge. More space was available after the removal of the broad gauge tracks through the station.

The greatest changes came in 1907 when a number of major improvements were made. A stone building was erected on the down platform containing a booking office, station master's office, waiting room and toilets, and the platforms were extended by 80 ft to the maximum length then possible between the road over-bridge to the west and the River Chew

bridge to the east (up side now 383 ft, down side 430 ft). Finally a roof was added to the open footbridge and new access provided, via steps, to Station Road on the town side of the road bridge. After completion of this work the impressive original up side building was used for little more than a parcels office and left luggage store: the station master's accommodation became vacant.

The last significant development took place in 1931 when the original Station Road bridge was replaced by a wider span steel structure. This allowed the platforms to be almost doubled in length westwards under the bridge and corrugated iron awnings were also provided. This gave the much needed extra capacity required for the Fry's workers trains and excursion trains (see below).

For seventy years from its opening in 1840, the main focus for station activity was passenger traffic, though some goods facilities were provided. From a short loading dock at the east end of the up platform a wagon turntable gave access to two sidings on a site on, and to the north of, the current car park. The wagon shunting was for many years undertaken by a horse. After much local pressure, a goods yard including a GWR red brick goods shed, cattle dock and pens and six ton crane opened on 16th January 1911 some half mile east of the station on the down side. Through the years this yard saw a great variety of goods traffic and private sidings were linked to a number of firms, some with their own wagons. Other sidings were laid on the up side, in particular in 1932 E. S. & A. Robinson opened a rail linked paper mill, movements included inwards pulp and coal and outwards the finished paper products. The traffic ceased in October 1969. The main goods yard closed in November 1965.

The early 1920s saw a key event for Keynsham Station. This was the construction and subsequent opening of J. S. Fry & Sons' new chocolate factory on a site at Somerdale, north west of Keynsham, to which it moved from its constricted site in central Bristol. A private rail link was built from the main line just east of the station and led to some two and a half miles of track serving the factory, coming into use first on 17th January 1925. A large amount of freight traffic was generated both during the construction phase and thereafter (eg cocoa beans/sugar in and chocolate products out) and passenger traffic also increased greatly. The GWR recognised this with the re-naming of the station, Keynsham and Somerdale, as from 1st February 1925. The station was used by many of the 4000 employees who had transferred from the central Bristol factory; not only did they use the normal services, but special Fry's workers' trains ran from the Bristol area. Such trains continued right up to the 1950s. No particular arrangements were made for workers who lived in the Bath area, the normal services appeared to suffice.

Gradually from the 1950s, travel by train dipped as the Somerdale employees increasingly lived in the Keynsham area or came by car. Moreover, the number of employees at the factory fell and many of the local stations in Bristol closed in the early 1960s. This led to first a cut back and then, by the early 1970s, the end of Fry's special trains. This in turn led to the dropping of Somerdale from the station name, as from 6th May 1974.

Another unusual aspect of Keynsham Station was the arrival, during the 1930s, and again after the Second World War, of excursion trains bringing visitors to tour the Fry's factory. Special trains were run from all over the country; in 1937 alone 113 such trains arrived carrying some 35,000 passengers. Over the period 1929-1938 some quarter of a million people travelled on the trips to the Bristol area centred on the Fry's factory. The visitors to the factory normally had refreshments there before being taken on coach tours of the Bristol/Bath area; almost always the return trains departed from Bristol Temple Meads. Finally each year a number of trade trains came to Keynsham bringing business people to the factory; there was also a Fry's exhibition train based at the factory that travelled to many parts.

With all this variety of traffic, passenger numbers at the station in the mid 1920s were around 100,000 and though this fell away in the 1930s, it rose again in the War when many evacuees still with jobs in Bristol, moved to live in Keynsham. A figure of some 125,000 was reached in 1941. Even in 1959 over 60,000 tickets were sold at Keynsham.

As with so many stations, decline set in rapidly during the mid 1960s and in October 1968 notices were issued proposing the closure of many stations in the area, including Keynsham. The last station master left in June 1965 and the station became unstaffed from 6th October 1969. In November 1969 the station was reprieved but physically it was neglected.

The principal buildings were demolished in June 1970 though the 1930s awnings at the west end were left; the footbridge had been dismantled the previous month and sold to the South Devon Railway and later re-erected at Buckfastleigh. In this sad state the

Keynsham. An excellent west facing view in about 1909. Note the large ornate covered footbridge bearing the emblems of the GWR.

station had a royal visit when, on 8th August 1977, the Queen boarded the royal train, having travelled by road from Bath.

Eventually revival came when a joint project, completed in December 1985, by British Rail and Avon County Council saw the installation of a new footbridge, a brick built shelter on the up platform and a much improved extended car park. Unfortunately the down platform was left without a shelter, though a small booking office, at first at the bottom of the footbridge steps and then later at the top by the road bridge, was installed to serve its developing role as a commuter station.

Today the station remains as at the 1985 revamp, with the up side shelter and the old 1930s corrugated shelters at the west end of the platforms. Numbers using the station are still reasonable, though somewhat reduced since the 1993 inauguration of the Brislington to central Bristol 'Park and Ride' scheme. The train service in the middle of the day is rather sparse but the morning and evening commuter services to and from Bath, Bristol and Bristol Filton Abbeywood (for the M.O.D. Procurement Division) are well patronised. The goods shed to the east remains. Having closed thirty seven years ago, it is now incorporated in an industrial area occupied by a stone firm and a transport contractor.

KINGSTON ROAD HALT

Weston, Clevedon & Portishead Light Railway (*see p 149*)

75

Langford. The station building on the north side of the single track Wrington Vale Light Railway.

LANGFORD

OPENED: 4th December 1901 (with the opening of the Wrington Vale Light Railway from Congresbury to Blagdon).

CLOSED: Passengers - 14th September 1931 (with closure of the Wrington Vale Light Railway to passenger traffic).

Goods - 1st November 1950 (with closure to goods traffic of the Wrington - Blagdon section).

Like many small rural stations, Langford was some distance from the village it served; in this case some half mile to the east on the north west side of the main A38. Level crossing gates controlled the traffic at this point and on the other side of the road was the station master's house, erected some two years after the station opening at a cost of £372. Sited on the north side of the track, the 150 ft long, 2 ft 6 inches high platform had a neat station building of red brick and timber with a zinc roof, very similar to those at Wrington and Blagdon. Here, as at Blagdon, a GWR style cast iron urinal was provided and a typical corrugated iron parcels shed.

Langford was the home of a Colonel Llewellyn, a director of the GWR in the 1900s, whose influence was sufficient to provide this remote location with a station! Not surprisingly the levels of passenger numbers were never great, declining from 7,085 in 1903 to 1,846 in 1923. After closure of the line to passengers in 1931, a camping coach was sited at Langford and another at Blagdon. A loop line and sidings served local freight traffic such as milk – some 5,000 churns were handled in 1903. During the Second World War the goods yard was a loading point for salvaged metal from the local area.

The station building was demolished in 1958. Remnants of the platform are still there and the station master's house is in residential use with major alterations and extensions. For many years a level crossing gate could still be seen in the road side hedge on the west side of the A38. However this gate has now been wrecked, apparently in a road accident, and any broken remains have now gone.

LANGPORT EAST

OPENED: 2nd July 1906 (on the Curry Rivel Junction - Somerton section of the GWR cut off route Castle Cary to Cogland Junction, originally opened through this site for freight traffic to and from the west on 12th February 1906).

CLOSED: Passengers and goods - 10th September 1962 (with withdrawal of local passenger services between Castle Cary and Taunton).

In 1906 the construction of the new west-east GWR mainline north of the town led to the opening of the second station at Langport, 53 years after Langport West had opened on the Taunton to Yeovil branch, south west of the town. Sited immediately east of the bridge over the Langport to Somerton road, Langport East was typical of the stations opened at this time on the GWR cut off route. The main building was on the down platform with a large canopy, whilst a brick shelter, also with canopy, served passengers on the up platform. The station was gas lit. A large covered footbridge linked the two platforms at the west end and a signal box stood at the Castle Cary end of the down platform. Attractive flower beds were a feature of the station. Edwardian

Langport East. A steam railmotor arriving from Taunton in about 1910. The main building is on the up platform (right).

gentry travelled from London to view peonies at the nearby Kelways Nurseries. In 1923 11,437 passenger tickets were issued, reducing to 5,513 in 1938.

No significant remnants of the station can now be seen, although the main building stood for over twenty years after closure. Former station railings and the base of a building can be seen adjacent to a road south of the station. A house is now built on the former site of the down platform and new houses are to the north of the line with a section of an old iron fence leading to the site of the up platform.

LANGPORT WEST

OPENED: Passengers - 1st October 1853 (with the opening to passenger traffic of the Durston - Hendford (Yeovil) branch from the Bristol & Exeter Railway).
Goods - 26th October 1853 (with the opening of the Durston - Hendford (Yeovil) branch to goods traffic).
CLOSED: Passengers - 15th June 1964 (with closure of the Taunton - Yeovil line to passenger traffic)
Goods - 6th July 1964 (with closure of the Taunton - Yeovil line to all traffic).

Sited at the south west of the town's main street, the station was well placed to generate a good level of passenger traffic. When opened it was called Langport, the West being added on 2nd July 1906 when the second town station, Langport East, opened north of the town on the new GWR cut off route Castle Cary to Cogland Junction (on the main Bristol - Taunton line).

The main Brunel type stone building with tall chimneys was on the up platform; in its early days it was completely surrounded by a canopy but later this was reduced covering the platform only. The down platform, longer than the up, had a waiting shelter. A footbridge was added at the west end in the 1920s, prior to this inter platform connections were via the road bridge. The original signal box was at the Yeovil end of the up platform; in 1906 a replacement box was sited on the down platform, also at the Yeovil end.

To the north east of the station, on the town side, beyond the forecourt, an extensive goods yard handled a variety of traffic. Facilities included a large warehouse. The goods shed, dock and cattle pens were adjacent to the up line, close to the Yeovil end of the platform. Over the years the whole station site and goods yard were prone to extensive flooding and

77

many photographs have been published illustrating passenger and goods trains braving the water.

Passenger numbers were relatively high. In 1913 30,376 tickets were issued, this number had fallen to 16,611 in 1923 and 12,506 in 1933. Though traffic was on the decline, some sixteen to nineteen staff worked at the station in the 1930s.

Today an industrial estate covers the whole area, the only significant remnant of railway days is the warehouse in the goods yard which, with extensions, is now appropriately called Great Western House. The road bridge over the original line at the north end of the station site also remains.

LODGE HILL

OPENED: 5th April 1870 (with the opening of the Cheddar - Wells section of the Cheddar Valley & Yatton Railway).

CLOSED: Passengers - 9th September 1963 (with closure of the Yatton - Witham line to passenger traffic). Goods - 10th June 1963.

Lodge Hill Station principally served the villagers of Westbury-sub-Mendip just to the north. The name

Langport West. A view south east towards Martock. A train stands at the up platform. At this early stage the horizontal canopy completely surrounds the building.

Lodge Hill. Looking east towards Wells. The attractive buildings display good examples of B & E architecture including the alternating roof tiles on the main building and the small cruciform motif along the ridge.

Westbury was not used because of possible confusion with the junction station of that name some thirty miles away in Wiltshire. The name derives from a small hillock some half mile south west of the station. The small attractive building and platform together with a goods shed, to the west, were on the north side of the single track line. The building was in the distinctive style of other B & E stations on the line, that is with patterned roof tiles, cruciform motifs on the roof ridge and decorative barge boards.

The form of the station and associated buildings remained largely unchanged throughout its 93 year life. Passenger ticket sales fell from 10,854 in 1903 to 5,575 in 1933.

Lodge Hill industrial estate now covers the site. The goods shed, with a small canopy, remains in use for industrial and office purposes but the station building has gone, some of the materials being used in the construction of the large new building at Cranmore for the East Somerset Railway. The adjoining road bridge also remains.

Long Ashton. An excursion train passes through in about 1937. The only known photograph of this small station west of Bristol.

path leading from the road on the up side. The estimated cost was £1,930. It is reported that some parcels traffic was handled. A suffix 'platform' was in use until 23rd September 1929. Sixty years after its closure, no traces remain.

LONG ASHTON

OPENED: 12th July 1926 (on the Bristol - Bridgwater section of the Bristol & Exeter Railway originally opened through the site in 1841).

CLOSED: 6th October 1941.

Sited immediately west of the Yanley Lane under bridge (and today almost under the Long Ashton By-Pass viaduct), this basic halt on the embankment had two 400 ft x 10 ft concrete platforms. A corrugated iron shelter and lamp hut were provided on the up platform and there was a small booking office on the

LONG SUTTON AND PITNEY

OPENED: 1st October 1907 (on the Curry Rivel Junction - Somerton section of the GWR cut off route Castle Cary to Cogland Junction originally opened through this site for freight traffic to and from the west on 12th February 1906).

CLOSED: Passengers - 10th September 1962 (with withdrawal of local passenger services between Castle Cary and Taunton).
Goods - 6th July 1964

This small station, located in a cutting west of a road over bridge in the hamlet of Upton, opened as a halt a year after through passenger services commenced on the line in July 1906. On 6th April 1908 the halt was re-designated a station. The settlements after

Long Sutton and Pitney. Looking west in the late 1950s from the bridge on the Long Sutton to Pitney road.

Lyng Halt. The small station on the original line of the Durston to Yeovil branch. Note the fire bucket on the side of the wooden shelter.

which the station is named are about a mile away to the south and north respectively. Corrugated iron buildings stood on both platforms, that on the up being a classic GWR pagoda hut. Paths and the road over-bridge connected the two platforms, which were lengthened in 1914. A small goods yard, opened in 1908, was sited on the up side and a signal box on the down side, both east of the road bridge. The box opened on 6th April 1908 and closed on 30th July 1964. In 1923 5,966 passenger tickets were issued but by 1933 this number had dropped to 3,328. For most of the 1930s there was a staff of two.

No remnants of the platforms or buildings survive but the former station house is in residential use on the Long Sutton side of the road bridge. Traces of fencing in the hedgerow indicate the possible location of the paths to the platform, whilst an old gate to the north of the bridge probably indicates the access to the goods yard.

LYNG HALT

OPENED: 24th September 1928 (on the Durston - Yeovil branch line originally opened through this site in 1853).
CLOSED: 15th June 1964 (with closure of the Taunton - Yeovil line to passenger traffic).

This halt opened on an original section of the Durston - Yeovil branch line which was by-passed by the Castle Cary - Cogland Junction cut off route in 1906. Sited in a cutting on the north side of the single

line, serving the villages of East and West Lyng, the halt comprised a single platform faced with wooden sleepers and a small timber shelter. Access was via a path leading from the north side of the road over bridge on the A361.

Remains of the gate can still be seen in the hedgerow, as can two concrete posts in the old cutting which could have carried the station name board.

MARSTON MAGNA

OPENED: 1st September 1856 (with the opening of the Frome - Yeovil section of the Wilts, Somerset & Weymouth Railway).
CLOSED: Passengers - 3rd October 1966.
Goods - 5th November 1962.

Marston Magna Station, sited about half a mile east of the village, off the minor road to Rimpton, was until 9th May 1895, named Marston. It was unusual in that no passing loop was provided at this point on the original single track broad gauge line between Castle Cary and Yeovil. Gauge conversion came at Marston in June 1874 and the line was doubled in 1881, a second platform then being added.

The station buildings were constructed of stone under slate roofs with the main buildings, including the station master's office, on the down (towards Yeovil) platform. A large shelter served passengers on the up platform. The platforms were some 290 ft long, but there was no footbridge. Inter-platform movements were via the Rimpton road bridge; access to the up platform was via a footpath and steps leading down from the bridge; to the down platform via the station approach road. A signal box stood at the Yeovil end of the up platform. The station master's house was sited on the station approach road at the Castle Cary end of the down platform. The station was lit by oil lamps until its closure. Passenger numbers were never high: 8,785 tickets issued in 1903, falling to 4,286 in 1933. Between the two World Wars, the annual Sunday School outing by train to Weymouth was very popular and Marston Magna was said to be practically deserted for the day.

Like many rural stations in Somerset, Marston Magna was a focus for much freight traffic, particularly before the competition from road transport. Freight and livestock was delivered to and taken from local traders and farms. Cattle arrived from Yeovil on market days and would then be driven to local farms. Cattle feed and horses were also handled. The station was unusual in that no sidings were ever laid on the up side, those on the down side comprised a dock siding and another longer siding. Coal arrived for the local creamery located behind the up platform. Local farmers brought milk to the creamery and, after processing, the milk churns were transferred to the station for rail haulage to London. The Magna Cider Company was also a regular rail customer, with huge cider casks arriving by rail.

During the Second World War Marston Magna Station was transformed when a large fan of sidings serving a huge ammunitions depot came into use on 16th December 1940. At first the Royal Engineers were based there but later in the War the United States Army had many hundreds of soldiers billeted in the village working at the depot. For long periods, particularly leading up to the D-Day Landings, train after train arrived with ammunition for the depot. This was unloaded onto lorries and stored all around the village area. Later in the War, large numbers of trains and lorries left Marston Magna for the embarkation sites. Soon after D-Day, the depot was emptied and life in the village and the station returned to normal, never to see such activity again. The sidings were taken out of use in November 1962 and the signal box closed on 16th February 1964. The station, having closed in October 1966, was completely demolished shortly after. The station master's house, with significant extensions, remains in residential use - the only reminder of the rail history of Marston Magna.

Marston Magna. A view south towards Yeovil, the principal buildings are on the down platform (left).

Martock. A view from the up platform towards Yeovil showing the staggered platforms. The principal building is on the down platform close to the level crossing over Martock's main street.

MARTOCK

OPENED: Passengers - 1st October 1853 (with the opening to passenger traffic of the Durston - Hendford (Yeovil) branch from the Bristol & Exeter Railway).
  Goods - 26th October 1853 (with the opening of the Durston - Hendford (Yeovil) branch to goods traffic).
CLOSED: Passengers - 15th June 1964 (with closure of the Taunton - Yeovil line to passenger traffic).
  Goods - 6th July 1964 (with closure of the Taunton - Yeovil line to all traffic).

Sited at the northern end of Martock's long main street, the station was well placed to attract high levels of passenger and goods traffic, particularly to Taunton. Passenger numbers were good: in 1913 32,865 tickets were issued but this halved by 1933 to 15,232. It is recorded that in 1877 the fare on the Saturday market train to the county town was 4/- 1st Class and 1/9 3rd Class. Sunday school outings by train became popular. Transport interchange was an early feature: the B & E timetable of 1877 stated that 'An omnibus meets every train - Fare 6d each to any part of the town'. The author recalls travelling to Martock by train with his parents for a short holiday in 1946.

The layout and facilities were relatively large for a branch line station. The two platforms were staggered, connected in later years by a footbridge (originally covered but then open) with the main buildings on the down (towards Taunton) platform adjacent to the level crossing and signal box. A large iron shed provided storage on the down platform for luggage conveyed by passenger trains. The up platform had a small wooden shelter. The nearby quarries on Ham Hill provided a mellow, yellow sandstone for buildings on the station site and goods yard. This goods yard was to the south of the station and handled local trade in cattle, coal, timber, building materials and also meat from the local abattoir. The goods shed and cattle pens were adjacent to, and west of, the down platform. There was a staff of fifteen in 1903, this had risen to nineteen by 1913. The Railway Hotel was close to the station on the village side.

Today a large industrial estate covers the whole station area, including the goods yard and former sidings which served the gas works. Isolated remnants of former buildings and walls remain as does the Railway Hotel on which a plaque records links with the old station and line.

Masbury. Looking north towards Radstock. All the main buildings are on the up platform, from left to right the station master's house, a signal box and the station building with booking office/waiting room.

MASBURY

OPENED: 20th July 1874 (with the opening of the Bath extension of the Somerset & Dorset Railway from Evercreech Junction to Bath).

CLOSED: Passengers - 7th March 1966 (with closure of the Bath Green Park - Poole line to passenger traffic).

Goods - 10th June 1963 (up siding taken out of use 1st July 1964).

Masbury, serving a largely rural community on the Mendips, was the highest station (750 ft) on the S & D line. The station became unstaffed as from 26th September 1938 and was re-designated Masbury Halt. The up platform housed virtually all the buildings with, from north to south, a substantial stone building containing a booking office and waiting rooms, a signal box and the large stone station master's house. The ground floor frontage of this house was surmounted by an unusual stone carving of an imaginary medieval castle and the Gothic legend 'Maesbury Castle'. Passengers on the down platform were only provided with a small wooden shelter. The road bridge just to the north, reached by steep paths, linked the two platforms.

A small goods yard with a cattle dock was on the up side of the line at the Shepton Mallet end whilst sidings on the down side, after serving a stone

crushing plant until 1928, were extended during the Second World War to serve a United States Army Camp. These sidings were lifted in 1959, whilst the up siding was taken out of use when the signal box closed on 1st July 1964.

The station master's house is now in residential use, 'Station House', with the platform and trackbed made into an attractive garden. The old station building is still in place, including the chimney, but in a derelict condition. Remains of a kissing gate at the top of the path to the down platform can still be seen.

MELLS ROAD

OPENED: 4th March 1887 (on the Radstock - Frome line, originally opened to coal traffic in 1854 and to passenger traffic in 1875).

CLOSED: Passengers - 2nd November 1959 (with closure of the Bristol - Radstock - Frome line to passenger traffic).

Goods - 15th June 1964.

After much local pressure placed on the GWR, this station opened some twelve years after the Radstock - Frome line had opened to passenger traffic. It opened as Mells, was re-named Mells Road on 16th November 1898 and finally relegated to halt status on 17th September 1956 when it became unstaffed. The renaming to Mells Road accurately reflected the local situation as the station was some two miles north west of the village. The main station building on the down (north) side of the line, although rather similar to those on the Bristol and

OPENED: 20th July 1874 (with the opening of the Bath extension of the Somerset & Dorset Railway from Evercreech Junction to Bath).

CLOSED: Passengers - 7th March 1966 (with closure of the Bath Green Park - Poole line to passenger traffic).

Goods - 10th June 1963.

Midford station was built into the hillside in an attractive situation overlooking the village itself. It was at the extreme southern end of a single track section of the S & D that started to the north at Bath Junction. South of the station and on the viaduct itself double track began and continued all the way to Radstock.

Unlike all the other stations on the Bath to Evercreech Junction section, the buildings were of wood. The principal building incorporated a booking office, a general waiting room and gent's urinal. In its early days a canopy was in place but this was later removed. A separate wooden hut accommodated the porters. The signal box at the southern end had a flat roof after 1936 following damage inflicted by a runaway train. A path from the platform up stone steps provided a more direct access to houses on the hill above the station. This led to the station master's house on Old Pack Horse Road. The goods yard at Midford was some distance away in the Bath direction where more space allowed the provision of two goods sidings, a goods shed and a six ton crane.

Following closure, dereliction set in and the station was demolished in December 1967. In the mid 1980s preservation attempts were commenced and through the years various work was carried out. The platform was cleared and resurfaced and the path to the houses above cleared. It was hoped that the station could be reconstructed and a heritage centre created. However, a visit in 2002 only revealed the cleared platform and path steps. The former trackbed immediately south of the station site and north of the viaduct is used as a car park for the Hope and Anchor public house.

North Somerset line, varied with a different style horizontal canopy and only two tall chimneys. A wooden building accommodating the gentlemen's toilets stood adjacent to, and east of, the main building. During 1909 both platforms were extended by an additional 90 ft; their full length becoming 288 ft. On the up side a new milk platform, a wooden waiting shelter and a corrugated iron lock up were also provided. A goods yard and shed to the west of the station off the up line served the local community with agricultural merchandise and accommodated movements of stone from the local quarries and coal from the many collieries.

The number of passengers handled was never great; passenger tickets issued fell from 8,864 in 1903 to 4,750 in 1933. Cheap tickets to Frome market were available on Wednesdays whilst on Saturday evenings cheap tickets were available for a night out in Bristol. Today although one of the tracks is still in place through the former station site, virtually all trace of the buildings has gone.

Above left Midford. Towards Bath, the principal wooden building still retains its attractive canopy.

Left Mells Road. A view in the late 1950s showing the principal building on the down (north) side of the line and the wooden waiting shelter on the up.

MIDSOMER NORTON AND WELTON

OPENED: 3rd September 1873 (with the opening of the Bristol & North Somerset Railway from Bristol to Radstock).

CLOSED: Passengers - 2nd November 1959 (with closure of the Bristol - Radstock - Frome line to passenger traffic).

Goods - 15th June 1964.

The station opened in 1873 as Welton and was renamed Welton and Midsomer Norton on 2nd May 1898. Finally, on 1st May 1904, it was renamed again as Midsomer Norton and Welton.

The station stood on the north side of the Bristol & North Somerset Railway's line to Radstock and came into operation with the line's opening in 1873. The main station building was the Bristol and North Somerset standard William Clarke design, incorporating a horizontal canopy with fretted valence, three tall chimneys and entrance to the building via the platform and a side wooden gate. The station also had a lean-to wooden building between the east end of the building and the gate and a small wooden signal cabin on the platform which later served as a parcels office. A goods shed stood west of the station building. A private siding west of the station served the North Somerset Brick and Tile Works, from 1926 to 1942. The siding was then extended and used by R. Blatchford and Co. until 1968 though goods traffic at the station itself ceased from 1964.

Local products dispatched from the station included milk in churns, timber buildings such as chalets, poultry houses and greenhouses from the local firm of Prattens, and printed materials such a cheque books from the Standard Cheque Works at Welton. Incoming goods included explosives (for use in the collieries) and cement; Blatchford's siding received steel and scrap metal. In the 1930s Midsomer Norton and Welton Station, although small, was a busy station serving the local community well. In 1933 24,500 passenger tickets were issued, 17,774 parcels forwarded and 4,383 general goods received.

Following closure to passengers in 1959 and to goods in 1964, deterioration set in and demolition was undertaken in August 1969 following a fire. Today only the eastern abutment of the road bridge east of the station remains as evidence of previous railway activity, together with the name Station Road.

Midsomer Norton and Welton. The main building, a good example of the William Clarke design used by the Bristol & North Somerset Railway. Note the large horizontal canopy and three tall chimneys.

MIDSOMER NORTON SOUTH (S & D)

OPENED: 20th July 1874 (with the opening of the Bath extension of the Somerset & Dorset Railway from Evercreech Junction to Bath).

CLOSED: Passengers - 7th March 1966 (with closure of the Bath Green Park - Poole line to passenger traffic).

Goods - 15th June 1964 (except some colliery sidings which closed 7th March 1966).

This S & D station was situated on Silver Street to the south of, and above, the town. Opening as Midsomer Norton, it was renamed Midsomer Norton and Welton on 16th October 1898 and remained as this until 26th September 1949 when the passenger station was renamed Midsomer Norton Upper and the goods depot Midsomer Norton South. Finally the passenger station was also given the suffix 'South' on 25th September 1950. A classic, attractive S & D station, it won 'Best Kept Station' awards for many years, particularly during the 1950s. The principal offices were sited on the down (south) platform close to the road. These included a booking office and hall, ladies' waiting room and station master's office. The neat building had the usual S & D canopy sloping down towards the line and two chimneys. The gentlemen's toilets and a further building for use by porters and for storage were also on the down platform behind which were goods sidings serving a goods shed, loading dock and cattle pens. The up platform passengers were

provided with a small wooden shelter of typical S & D design with a small upward sloping canopy. The signal box stood alongside the station garden behind the up platform; for some years a greenhouse was a feature in the garden. The station mainly served the local community, both for passengers and goods. Many of the photographs of this station feature large numbers of milk churns.

Today the station is in remarkably good condition. In the 1990s the station underwent a period of restoration when an Avon County Council Youth Training Programme took over the task initially started as a school project in the 1970s. The former goods shed was converted into a woodworking shop. Until sold in 1995, it formed part of Norton Radstock College Department of Art and Design.

When visited in early 2002 there were clear signs of activity associated with the new Somerset & Dorset Railway Heritage Trust's restoration and short railway project. The Trust has secured a lease on the station buildings from Bath and North East Somerset Council. It is hoped to turn the station into a working museum and re-lay track towards Chilcompton on which steam trains can run again. The two platforms, main buildings, shelter and goods shed remain and a fresh section of line has been laid on which a couple of wagons stand. It is certainly the best surviving example of a S & D small station and, but for its signal box, is still complete.

MILBORNE PORT

OPENED: 7th May 1860 (with the opening of the Gillingham - Sherborne section of the Salisbury & Yeovil Railway operated by the London & South Western Railway).

CLOSED: Passengers - 7th March 1966.
Goods - 6th November 1961.

Located about one mile north of Milborne Port, the main buildings on the down (south) side of the line included the station master's house. The house incorporated round headed windows characteristic of buildings on the line. A signal box was added in 1875 on the down platform; a small extension was added to the box as late as 1960 so that tickets could be purchased from the signalman. A notice on the side of the box stated 'Obtain tickets at the signal box' – a practice linked to the withdrawal of staff, except the signalman, and the station's demotion to the status of a halt on 6th November 1961.

Up platform passengers were served by only a small brick built shelter; the two platforms were connected by an open steel footbridge at the Sherborne end. Passenger numbers were never high at Milborne Port; in 1928 7,312 passenger tickets

Milborne Port. Towards Sherborne and Yeovil. The station master, signalman, booking clerk and three porters pose in this early photograph.

were issued, in 1936 the number was 4,634.

Two pairs of railway staff cottages were sited behind either end of the up platform and a small goods yard on the down side towards Sherborne provided limited facilities including cattle pens. The yard closed on 6th November 1961 with the withdrawal of station staff.

The signal box closed on 21st June 1965, just under a year before the station completely closed in March 1966. The station buildings have been converted into two houses, the two pairs of staff cottages continue in residential use and the up platform survives, though somewhat overgrown.

MILTON ROAD HALT

Weston, Clevedon & Portishead Light Railway (see p 149)

MILVERTON

OPENED: 8th June 1871 (with the opening of the Norton Junction - Wiveliscombe section of the Devon & Somerset Railway).

CLOSED: Passengers - 3rd October 1966 (with closure of the Norton Fitzwarren - Barnstaple line).
Goods - 30th September 1963 (with closure of the Barnstaple line to goods traffic).

Sited north of the village, the station was the first on the Taunton - Barnstaple branch line after it left the main GWR line at Norton Junction. Milverton was apparently the focal point of celebrations when the first section of the line opened to Wiveliscombe in June 1871. Many of the residents of Wiveliscombe went to Milverton which was elaborately decorated. By the turnpike gate was a double arch with 'Success to the Devon & Somerset Railway' worked in flowers and other arches also displayed messages. Two bands played, rural sports were held. Sixty quarter pound packets of tea were given to the oldest and poorest women in the parish and the pupils of the National School (nearly three hundred) each received a penny. The leading citizens of both Milverton and Wiveliscombe were taken to Taunton

Milverton. A Taunton bound train at the up platform. The signal box replaced an earlier small wooden box on the same site. The up side waiting shelter is identical to that at Axbridge.

in a saloon carriage and entertained in a marquee.

Milverton was originally a single platform station but in 1880 an up platform and crossing loop were added. This loop was extended in 1925 and 1936. The simple brick built station was on the down platform, dating from broad gauge days. A small signal box, goods shed and a coal siding were also provided on the down side. On the up platform, the timber waiting shelter, of typical B & E design with decorative barge boards, was identical to that at Axbridge. In 1903 a larger signal box and a goods yard, to the west of the station, were provided, both on the down side. Inward traffic was chiefly coal, fertilisers and livestock; outward traffic was principally sugar beet.

All traces of the station have now gone, with the trackbed west of this point now part of a new alignment of the B3227 by-passing Milverton. Only Station Road remains. Of interest is that the flower beds on the Station Road/by-pass roundabout are enclosed with old railway sleepers!

MINEHEAD

OPENED: 16th July 1874 (with the opening of the Minehead Railway from Minehead to Watchet).

CLOSED: Passengers - 4th January 1971 (with closure of the Norton Fitzwarren - Minehead line).

Goods - 6th July 1964.

REOPENED: 28th March 1976 (with the reopening of the Minehead - Blue Anchor section of the restored West Somerset Railway).

Minehead. A GWR pagoda hut providing extra shelter in about 1920. The main building was extended west over the site of the hut in the early 1930s.

At the opening of the Minehead Railway in 1874, the station, costing some £1100, consisted of one platform on which stood a stone building with canopy. A stone built goods shed was sited opposite the platform. By the early 1900s significant increases in traffic led to the provision of a second platform face, more sidings and a signal box at the east end. These were brought into use on 1st July 1905. Also about this time the GWR also erected one of its pagoda style corrugated iron huts adjacent to the north west (town) end of the station building. In the mid 1920s the pagoda hut was removed, its site being taken by a major extension of the station building itself. An awning at the town end was also added later.

In 1934, in connection with the doubling of the track from Dunster, a further re-modelling of the station was undertaken. The platforms were lengthened from 745 to 1250 ft towards Dunster. Now about a quarter of a mile long, they were then able to accommodate sixteen coach trains. A 200 ft long canopy over both platforms was added beyond the east end of the station building. Run round loops were installed for each platform, together with extra carriage sidings. A new tall wooden signal box and large water tower were built at the east end of the station site.

Extensive goods facilities were in operation in the mid 1930s on both sides of the passenger station.

The original large goods shed, dock and cattle pens were on the sea (north) side whilst to the south was the original engine shed, a 45 ft turntable, carriage and goods sidings. These sidings served local builders and coal merchants as well as the adjacent cattle market and abattoir. The engine shed closed in November 1956 and the signal box on 27th March 1966. Soon after the box was demolished. Goods facilities were withdrawn generally in July 1964.

When the West Somerset Railway took over the station site in 1975 the old goods shed was converted into a locomotive depot and workshop; this conversion included the digging of a pit down its entire length thus enabling staff to work under the locomotives. The former goods office at the town end was converted into a staff mess room; in 1999 a major extension was added at the east end of the shed and general restoration took place.

Much renovation and conversion work has been undertaken to the now listed station building, with the former booking office, waiting and staff rooms being converted into offices for the West Somerset Railway itself. These include a small passenger information office and the station master's office. The former parcels office is now the station shop. A new booking office has been constructed at the town end of the building incorporating fittings brought from Cardiff Central Station. This office was refurbished in 1997. Vintage style lighting has replaced the former British Rail fluorescent tubes.

In 1976, in order to enhance water supplies for the locomotives, a water tower for the platform was purchased from British Rail and brought from Pwllheli in North Wales. This remained in use until 1996 when it was no longer adequate to provide water for the larger locomotives now operating the West Somerset Railway. It was subsequently dismantled in 1999 and sold to the Welshpool and Llanfair Light Railway where it is now in use at Welshpool itself.

In the early 1990s a major revision of the track layout and signalling took place associated with the construction of the new Minehead relief road connecting the A39 to the sea front near the Butlins complex. This included the installation of an automatic controlled level crossing over the new road and the commissioning of the signal box that had been brought to Minehead from Dunster in 1977. In 1991 the West Somerset Railway built a new carriage and wagon works at the east end of the site on the sea side of the platform.

Much of the former goods yard to the south of the

Monkton Combe. The station staff with a number of gangers gathered on the platform to mark the station's opening in 1910.

station is now used as a large car park (the site of a market on some days) and an industrial estate, including a major development for Travis Perkins.

MONKTON COMBE

OPENED: 9th May 1910 (with the opening of the Camerton - Limpley Stoke line).

CLOSED: Passengers - 21st September 1925 (with closure of the Hallatrow - Limpley Stoke line to passenger traffic).
Goods - 15th February 1951 (with closure of the Hallatrow - Limpley Stoke line).
Temporary closure to passengers 22nd March 1915 and to goods traffic 1st April 1918 as a war time measure; reopened for passengers and goods 9th July 1923.

The platform was sited to the north side of the line on Station Road (now Mill Lane), in the valley below the village of Monkton Combe. The station, a basic wooden structure with a small canopy and two chimneys, had a booking office, general waiting room, ladies' waiting room with toilet and a gentlemen's toilet. There was also a corrugated iron lamp hut and attractive flower beds on the platform.

To the north of the station was Monkton Combe School; to the south a mill belonging to Messrs T.R. Freeman and Sons, and these two establishments were key customers. The mill produced flock for mattress fillings, much of which was dispatched to the north of England. Rags and teasels for the mill arrived by rail as did wagons of coal both for the mill and local coal merchants. In 1920 some 2000

tons of goods were handled at Monkton Combe.

At the beginning and end of each term the School made great use of the railway - a private lorry took luggage to and from the station. It was usual for three covered railway vans to be loaded with trunks, tuck boxes and cycles destined respectively for London, Bristol and destinations on the Southern Railway. An extra porter from Bath would be sent to help at these times, supplementing the staff of station master and one porter.

Just as Camerton, along the Cam Valley line, had featured in the 1931 film, 'The Ghost Train', Monkton Combe was the locality for filming 'The Titfield Thunderbolt' in 1952. The station was renovated and renamed Titfield. The canopy was extended and a new external ticket window constructed. The station was also provided with a number of period details such as weighing and chocolate machines but, when filming finished, all the extra details were removed and the station returned to its original state. It lasted another six years before demolition in 1958. The station site remained open but derelict for some years until the land was taken over and raised for Monkton Combe's new all weather sports pitch in the late 1970s.

Today the only remains of the station are two black painted gateposts either side of a modern garage on the east side of Mill Lane. These were the gateposts of the road entrance to Monkton Combe Station. Close by stands No 1 Station Cottages. The sports pitch completely covers the station site.

Montacute. A Taunton to Yeovil train arrives at the station in 1963, a year before it closed to passengers.

MONTACUTE

OPENED: 1882 (on the Durston- Yeovil (Hendford) branch originally opened through this site in 1853).
CLOSED: Passengers - 15th June 1964 (with closure of the Taunton - Yeovil line to passenger traffic). Goods - 30th September 1963.

The station, the last to open on the branch line in 1882, served the nearby village and its magnificent mansion. The neat station building with a canopy stood on the south west side of the single track line. In later years concrete components replaced the original wooden platform structure. A goods shed with a dock stood at the Yeovil end on the down side of the line. Cattle pens were provided between the platform and the shed. A signal box, opened on 6th March 1908, replaced the earlier 1882 box which was sited opposite the goods shed. A station master's house was provided east of the line, although somewhat isolated from the station itself. Passenger numbers fell from a peak in 1923 when 16,423 tickets were issued to 4,808 ten years later.

The use of the track formation for the new A3088 link road from Yeovil to the A303 at Cartgate roundabout has obliterated all traces of the station though the station master's house survives. Concrete sections of the Montacute platform were used to construct Doniford Beach Halt on the West Somerset Railway.

NAILSEA AND BACKWELL

OPENED: 14th June 1841 (with the opening of the Bristol - Bridgwater section of the Bristol & Exeter Railway).

CLOSED: Passengers - remains open for services on the Bristol - Weston-Super-Mare - Taunton line. Goods - 1st July 1964.

Opening as Nailsea, this was one of the original stations on the B & E Railway when the first section opened to Bridgwater in June 1841. Sited on a high embankment some 40 ft above road level and midway between the settlements of Nailsea to the north and Backwell to the south, the principal buildings that served the station for many years are believed to have been constructed in about 1860. The main stone building on the up (Nailsea) side included the booking and waiting room facilities with shelter being provided by a small canopy over the two large bay windows. Behind the west end of this up platform stood a wooden goods shed with sliding doors and beyond it a small signal box. Together with a small box on the down side, to the west of the station, it controlled cross over lines and short sidings at each end of the station. By contrast, the down platform was only provided with a small wooden shelter bearing the characteristic B & E decorative barge boards.

Because of its siting on an embankment it was necessary to use relatively lightweight materials and thus, for many years, the platforms rested on timber supports for most of their length. These were later replaced by brick and concrete. Inter-platform movements were via footboards at the west end of the platform until 1907, when an open metal footbridge was installed, manufactured by Finch & Co of Chepstow.

The station name changed to Nailsea and Backwell on 1st May 1905 but reverted to Nailsea on 6th May 1974. Today, however, the full Nailsea and Backwell appears on the nameboard and the station has a good service, including local trains on the Bristol to Taunton line and limited through inter-city services to London Paddington. In the mid 1980s major refurbishment took place; although the old down side shelter remained intact, the principal buildings on the up side had been demolished by that time. A new car park was constructed. Today the original foundations of the up side buildings are still to be seen but modern shelters stand on the two platforms, the original wooden shelter on the down side now gone. Indicative of the dominance of passenger movement into Bristol are the three shelters on the up side, two being combined with a small booking office manned at peak times. The down side platform has only one shelter.

Nailsea and Backwell. A close up view on 6th October 1962 of the fine up side building with bay windows.

Nightingale Valley Halt. A rare photograph of this short lived halt in the Avon Gorge below the Clifton Suspension Bridge.

NIGHTINGALE VALLEY HALT

OPENED: 9th July 1928 (on the Portishead branch originally opened through this site in 1867).
CLOSED: 12th September 1932.

During the 1920s the GWR sought to develop the volume of passenger traffic on the Portishead branch, particularly day trippers. As part of this campaign, a halt was opened for summer services only below the Suspension Bridge in the Avon Gorge. Constructed mainly of old railway sleepers and with a small iron passenger shelter, it only served passengers for five summers from July 1928 to September 1932. With the shortest life of any station or halt in Somerset, its provision was described by the main historian of the Portishead branch, Mike Vincent, as 'an almost complete failure'. Today no trace remains.

NORTON FITZWARREN

OPENED: 1st June 1873 (on the Taunton - Beam Bridge section of the Bristol & Exeter Railway originally opened through this site in 1843).
CLOSED: Passengers - 30th October 1961.
  Goods - 6th July 1964 (except for private siding).

Located at the end of Station Road, south of the village, Norton Fitzwarren had an eventful history. A junction on the GWR main Bristol - Exeter line for the Minehead branch had been sited here, two miles west of Taunton, since 1862, but the station was not built and opened until 1st June 1873. This was about two months after the first section of the Devon & Somerset Railway to Wiveliscombe had opened, branching off the Minehead line just west of Norton Junction. When opened, and until quadrupling of the track at this point, it was a two platform station with the main stone building, without a canopy, on the up line. The buildings and also a smaller wooden shelter on the down platform incorporated typical B & E decorative features with barge boards and cruciform roof tiles. Goods sidings were provided on the up side at the Taunton end whilst the station master's house and Railway Hotel were also sited on the up side at the end of Station Road. A fine covered footbridge connected the two platforms.

Complete rebuilding took place associated with the 1931/2 quadrupling of the main line from Cogland Junction to Norton Fitzwarren. Very slightly east of the original site, the new station included two island platforms serving the four tracks, connected by a long lattice open footbridge. It came into use on

Norton Fitzwarren. The main station buildings, with B & E barge boards and ridge tiles, on the up platform of the original 1873 station.

Norton Fitzwarren. Looking east towards Taunton in 1961 showing the two 1931 island platforms on the four track line.

2nd December 1931. Both platforms now had large timber shelters with surrounding canopies. The principal station offices for both passenger and goods were in two buildings on the up side at the end of Station Road, separated from the platforms by the up relief line. Major changes were also made to the trackwork and a new signal box was provided by the down line opposite the station, opening in February 1932.

From relatively small beginnings Norton Fitzwarren had changed into a major junction station complex. Despite this junction position, it is doubtful whether many passengers ever changed at the station, as the Barnstaple and Minehead trains virtually always started and terminated at Taunton. However the goods yard, with its small goods shed, was often busy handling large quantities of cider apples from orchards in the area; other agricultural traffic was also handled using the relatively few sidings available.

From 1959 decline began with the station closing to passengers in 1961 and to goods, apart from a private siding, in 1964. The end came with the closure of the signal box on 1st March 1970.

Now it is hard to believe that such a railway complex ever existed. At the end of Station Road (the only clue to the rail activity) a tall wire fence runs along the main west of England line and no trace of the buildings can be seen. The goods yard, occupied for some years by Taunton Cider, is now derelict, only the former Railway Hotel still exists, boarded up and dilapidated. A long public footbridge spanning the railway and sidings just east of the station is still in place.

OLDFIELD PARK

OPENED: 18th February 1929 (on the Bristol Temple Meads - Bath Spa section of the GWR Bristol to London line originally opened through this site in 1840).
CLOSED: Remains open for passenger services on the Bristol - Bath line.

In 1920 Bath City Council suggested to the GWR that a station should be opened at Brook Road, to serve a suburb of the city that had developed greatly since the coming of the railway. The proposed site was a little up the hill away from the rival services of the Bath Tramways. Staffed by one porter, Oldfield Park Station opened with a wooden ticket office at the head of the steps to the down platform and two corrugated iron arc-roofed shelters on each platform. During the 1970s the station became unmanned and its iron shelters were replaced by bus stop type shelters. In 1988 the Friends of Oldfield Park Station successfully campaigned for a better service and in 1994 the station was refurbished and made accessible for the disabled by ramped steps.

The presence today of two shelters on the down platform (towards Bristol) and only one on the up (towards Bath) indicates the principal direction of travel. In 1986 an average of 120 passengers per day used the station; by 1999 this had risen to 440. It is now a relatively well used small suburban station, with an average of some twenty five trains stopping daily in each direction.

Oldfield Park. A view towards Bath in 1951; two corrugated iron shelters provide cover on each platform.

Paulton Halt. A rare eastward view of a halt that was only used for two short periods.

PAULTON HALT

OPENED: 5th January 1914 (on the Hallatrow - Camerton originally opened through this site in 1882).

CLOSED: 21st September 1925. Temporary closure 22nd March 1915 - 9th July 1923, originally as a war time measure.

Close to the locality known locally as Gossard Bridge, where the Paulton to High Littleton road crosses the Camerton - Limpley Stoke line, the GWR opened a halt south west of the bridge in 1914. Constructed of hard packed stone with a brick facing and surfaced with gravel, the 3 ft high platform on the north side of the line was 150 ft long and 8 ft wide with a nameboard and three lamp standards. The usual oil lighting was provided and passenger access was via a footpath from the road, north of the bridge. Some form of shelter may have been provided but no photographic evidence exists. No staffing was ever provided. It is extremely doubtful whether many passengers ever used the halt. It was some way north of Paulton itself and potential passengers to the north and west would probably have used the larger stations of Hallatrow and Clutton if travelling to Bristol, as no change of train would have been necessary. Passenger services were suspended during the First World War and then only resumed for the short period 1923 to 1925. No remains of this halt can now be traced, though steps down and a gap in the fence probably mark the point where the station footpath left the road.

PENSFORD

OPENED: 3rd September 1873 (with the opening of the Bristol & North Somerset Railway from Bristol to Radstock).

CLOSED: Passengers - 2nd November 1959 (with closure of the Bristol - Radstock - Frome line to passenger traffic).

Goods - 15th June 1964 (except for private siding).

Pensford Station was sited close to the north end of the village and access was via 'Station Approach' which left the A37 just north of the rail overbridge. The impressive Pensford Viaduct was to the south of the station and goods yard.

The main building, on the up (west) side, was a classic example of the standard William Clarke design used at stations on the Bristol & North Somerset Railway between Bristol and Radstock. This design, also found on other West Country lines (eg the Abbotsbury branch in Dorset) involved a principal brick built structure with a large fretted horizontal canopy and three tall chimneys. The booking office and waiting room were incorporated in the main building, whilst toilets were provided in a small adjacent structure. Access to the platform, booking office and waiting room was via a gate at the side of the building and not through the building itself. The down side platform was provided with a small wooden shelter with a fretted canopy. The platforms were extended in 1898.

The goods yard with goods shed was sited south of the station on the up side; the yard remained in use until June 1964 but a loop line through the station

Pensford. A view north in the mid 1950s of the up platform, including the classic William Clarke design station building and the 1898 signal box.

had been removed earlier in 1960. An early signal box, opened in 1873, was replaced by a new box at the south end of the up platform in 1898. This remained in use until goods traffic ceased in 1964. In 1965 the box and goods shed were demolished.

The whole station site has been developed as a housing estate and little trace of its former use can be seen apart from the nearby embankments of the railway line. However 'Station House', on Station Approach, still remains in residential use.

PILL

OPENED: 18th April 1867 (with the opening of the Portishead branch from the Bristol - Exeter line).

CLOSED: Passengers - 7th September 1964 (with closure of the Bristol - Portishead branch to passenger traffic).

Goods - 10th June 1963.

Sited in a cutting close to the centre of the old settlement of Pill, the station opened with the Portishead branch in 1867. The main station building was built on Station Road adjacent to the road bridge and above the platforms at their eastern end. These platforms were extended first in January 1880 and again in 1912. A signal box was built on

Pill. A railmotor from Portishead to Bristol at the up platform in about 1910.

the down platform at the end of the First World War. Basic brick shelters were provided on both platforms.

The loop line through the station was extended at both ends as from 7th March 1912; at the same time a small goods yard with goods shed was opened at the Portishead end on the up side. These goods facilities were used extensively in both World Wars. During the Second World War the station staff consisted of a station master, two porters and two signal women. Passenger traffic was generally of a reasonable level, principal users being commuters both up the line to Bristol and down to Portishead docks and industries. Travellers using the Pill ferry from Shirehampton regularly made their way to the station for onward rail travel. As at other stations on the branch, War evacuees from Bristol were regular commuters into the city's factories and offices.

The station buildings on Station Road remain, now in commercial use, and remnants of both platforms can still be seen. A single track has been re-laid through the site of the former station for freight services to and from Royal Portbury Dock.

POLSHAM HALT

OPENED: December 1861 (on the Glastonbury - Wells section of the Somerset Central Railway originally opened through this site in 1859).

CLOSED: Passengers and goods - 29th October 1951.

The Glastonbury - Wells line originally had no intermediate station, but even before its opening two petitions were submitted by the villagers of Coxley requesting a station. However, a decision was taken to site a station at Polsham, a scattered farming community about a mile south west of Coxley, possibly because some of the land acquired for the branch belonged to the family of Polsham House. The line passed conveniently close to the house and a gate in the brick wall gave direct access to the station!

It was a neat, compact station on the east of the single track line. The 200 ft length platform housed a red brick building built in 1894 and a short siding was located opposite the station. A cement-faced station master's house was erected at the south end of the platform in the 1920s; this necessitated the re-positioning of the small signal box, that also worked the level crossing gates, to a site next to the crossing.

Polsham Halt. Photographed before the building of the station master's house at the south end of the platform.

Passenger traffic was limited at Polsham but the local agricultural community was served well by the goods facilities; at one time a goods train called every day. It was formally re-designated as a halt in July 1938.

Fifty years after closure the station house is still in residential use with station seats (GWR) and a signal in the garden. One of the original level crossing gate posts also remains.

PORTBURY

OPENED: 18th April 1867 (with the opening of the Portishead branch from the Bristol - Exeter line).

CLOSED: Passengers and goods - 30th April 1962.

Portbury Station, some half mile north of the village, opened with the branch in 1867 at a site just east of the road bridge carrying the original A369 Bristol to Portishead road via Sheepway. Today this section of the road has been replaced by the more direct road to Portishead. The impressive building (which still remains in use today as 'Station House') was south of the line, incorporating the main station offices and a station master's house. For a period Portbury was a main crossing point on the branch via a loop line; a second platform served passengers on trains using this loop. However for most of its life it was a single

Portbury. The large building incorporating the main station offices and the station master's house.

Portbury Shipyard. The only known photograph of the wooden platform and shelter serving workers at the nearby Admiralty establishment from 1918 to 1923.

platform (extended in 1890) and opposite the buildings a special feature was the station garden, including impressive examples of topiary. To the east of, and behind, the station a short siding served local goods traffic, in particular a cattle dock. The cattle movements were associated with a cattle market held in Portbury village. Horse boxes were a feature of local traffic and records also show that for some years open wagons took pit props away from Portbury. Such goods traffic always seems to have been equally important to passenger movements which were never large at Portbury. In later years the station master was only assisted by one other member of staff. Today a rusty single track still passes under the old station bridge but this, and indeed the whole formation, is well hidden by undergrowth and brambles.

PORTBURY SHIPYARD

OPENED: 16th September 1918 (between Pill and
  Portbury on the Portishead branch originally opened
  through this site in 1867).
CLOSED: 26th March 1923.

In July 1917 Parliament approved the establishment of a National Shipyard Company, whose purpose was to ensure the rapid replacement of ships lost to enemy action. These new shipyards were all proposed in the Bristol Channel at Beachley, Chepstow and Portbury, though the last was actually sited at Sheephouse Farm, Easton-in-Gordano. Ship fitting facilities were to be developed at Avonmouth, and thus the nearest shipyard at Portbury was chosen for the new company's management offices. All this activity brought significant volumes of traffic to the Portishead branch. The site of the proposed shipyard was connected to the branch line and at the junction a loop line, siding, signal box and small passenger station were built. Constructed of wood with a timber shelter, the station was a short distance west of the Duck Lane road bridge, leading to Sheephouse Farm.

With end of the War the shipyard project was abandoned. At one time some 1800 men had been based at a vast camp at Sheephouse but even with the major project ending, the Portbury site continued as an important centre for Admiralty civilian personnel. This in itself justified the presence of the small station and for just under five years it served both troop and passenger trains. The return fare to Portbury Shipyard from Bedminster was 6d.

No trace of the former station building can now be seen but rusty track still passes through the station site.

PORTISHEAD

FIRST STATION

OPENED: 18th April 1867 (with the opening of the Portishead branch from the Bristol - Exeter line).

CLOSED: Passengers and goods - 4th January 1954 (with the take-over of the site for the new Portishead B Power Station - replaced by second station).

SECOND STATION

OPENED: 4th January 1954 (replacing the first station).

CLOSED: Passengers - 7th September 1964 (with closure of the Portishead branch to passenger traffic).
Goods - 1st May 1967 (apart from private siding which closed on 3rd April 1981).

The history of Portishead Station and the associated traffic, both passenger and freight, was linked closely with other features of Portishead's life - the pier, the docks and the power stations.

Under the provisions of the Bristol and Portishead Pier and Railway Company Acts of 1863 and 1866, the broad gauge Portishead branch from the GWR line west of Bristol and the first Portishead Station opened in April 1867. The pier, also authorised by the Acts, opened in June 1868; the branch itself was converted to standard gauge in January 1880.

The impressive brick built 1867 station was located at the far end of Station Road some half mile north of High Street. To reach the station, trains crossed a wooden viaduct constructed over the Portishead Pill. The station buildings included a fine canopy over the single platform, a large booking hall with an adjacent booking office, a general waiting room, a ladies waiting room with toilet; gentlemen's toilets and offices for goods and parcels. Accommodation for the station master was also incorporated. Over the years the station was a social centre for this northern part of Portishead - the station bar was, at various times, patronised by dockers, power station workers and local residents as well as rail passengers.

Some five years after the station opening, work commenced on the building of Portishead Docks; much traffic was generated on the branch and at the station itself. The docks opened in April 1879. Although the import of materials for dock construction generated traffic, the twelve years gap between the opening of the branch and the docks meant that freight traffic was slow to develop and records suggest that up until about 1876 much of the goods traffic arriving at Portishead Station was carried on passenger trains. Indeed in its early history more traffic was probably generated by activities at Portishead pier with passengers travelling to and from the steamers which called en route to other Bristol Channel ports and resorts.

This leads to the subject of Portishead's second early station - the Pier Station. As its name suggest, this was built close to the pier, opening in the late 1870s. It seems likely that the Pier Station was used almost entirely for freight traffic. If ever isolated

Portishead. An excellent photograph of the original 1867 station, the large building with canopy including accommodation for the station master.

passenger trains served the Pier Station, this probably ceased entirely after 1884 when regular steamer services no longer called at Portishead Pier. However, the Pier Station building survived for many years and was only demolished along with other buildings in the old station and pier area in 1954 with the construction of the Portishead B Power Station.

The next key factor in the life of Portishead Station was the construction and opening of Portishead A Power Station. Sited to the west of the station at the foot of the hill, it opened in 1929. Its construction, like that of the docks earlier, created much traffic, whilst, once open, the fuel needs and the workers themselves brought both freight and passenger traffic to the branch line and station.

In the 1920s and 1930s the GWR took initiatives to encourage more passenger traffic on the Portishead branch. Traditional seaside holidays had revived after the First World War and Campbell Steamers called regularly at the pier once more. An intensive passenger service was run on the line, mostly hourly but sometimes half hourly, serving leisure trips to the town (and steamers), commuters to Bristol's factories and offices and children to Bristol's schools. The GWR itself started a bus service from Portishead Station to Redcliffe Bay, later superseded by a service run by the Bristol Omnibus Company. The increased business prompted an expansion of the station - an original carriage loop was converted into a passenger train run round loop and a new second platform serving this loop came into use on 9th March 1930, in time for the Easter and summer season traffic.

Business at Portishead Station remained good through the 1930s until the inevitable dip with the outbreak of war. As in the First World War, freight traffic on the branch, in particular to the docks, was given priority over passenger trains. However, although leisure movements decreased, commuter movements increased, with many evacuees who had been moved for safety out to the Pill and Portbury areas travelling to work in the factories of the Ashton/Bedminster areas of Bristol.

The first station site was taken over in the 1950s with the construction and opening of Portishead B Power Station, situated between the A Power Station and the docks. This necessitated the building of a new station some half a mile south at the other end of Station Road and required demolition of a number of buildings, including the local Labour Exchange and a British Legion hut. The new site was

Portishead. The second station which served the town for ten years from 1954 to 1964.

almost identical to one originally proposed for a Portishead terminus when plans were being drawn up for the branch in the early 1860s, though the 1867 station was actually built nearer to the proposed pier and the planned future docks.

The last trains to use the 1867 station were the 8.10 a.m. from Bristol and 9.05 a.m. from Portishead on 4th January 1954. Following the departure of the 9.05 to the sound of detonators, station staff transferred themselves and equipment to the new station where the first train to arrive was the 12.11 p.m. from Temple Meads.

Built of pre-stressed concrete and local limestone, the new station, costing some £250,000 contributed by the Generating Board, was luxurious compared with the old. Set back from Station Road, on a semi circular drive, the main building incorporated the booking hall/office and offices for the station master and porter. Behind the main building a two face platform 35 ft wide and 750 ft long was covered for most of its length (600 ft) by a flat roof of concrete and glass. Facilities on the platform included a general waiting room, ladies' waiting room and toilets for gentlemen and ladies. The waiting rooms were floored with rubber tiles and heated by marble effect Parkray heaters, much in vogue at the time. In March 1954 the new station was even featured in *The Architect* which commented on the new comfortable seats!

The opening of the new station brought considerably increased use by passengers, encouraged both by the improved facilities and the proximity of the station to the town centre. A wide range of goods traffic was catered for in a large goods yard with a capacity for 300 wagons. In the early 1950s the yard handled construction materials for the B Power Station and a new factory for Albright & Wilson. After these two major projects were complete freight traffic still continued at a relatively high level with both general goods for the town and its industries and coal for the power station.

Soon after the station opened subsidence problems began, unsurprisingly, it being built on ash laid upon re-claimed land. By 1955 a cure was claimed but in reality problems continued until its closure. During the early 1960s steam trains were replaced by diesel cars, and services were reduced. Nevertheless business remained good on peak days. Whit Monday 1963, just a year before closure, saw over 400 passengers travel to Portishead for the day on the morning train. Although final closure of the line and the station was delayed from February because of impact upon summer holiday movements, the last passenger train ran on 7th September 1964. (The author and his future wife were on board.)

The fight to keep passenger services had failed. Nevertheless campaigning continued and this was re-enforced in 1965 when planning permission was sought to convert the former station booking hall and forecourt into a petrol filling station. However, plans were approved and Station Garage opened in October 1966. For some years the former main building survived as part of the garage but recent re-development included complete demolition of the station building. The campaign to restore passenger services on the line to Portishead continues, particularly now that a long section of the branch has been re-laid for use by heavy freight traffic to and from Royal Portbury Dock.

PORTISHEAD

Weston, Clevedon & Portishead Light Railway (*see p 150*)

PORTISHEAD SOUTH

Weston, Clevedon & Portishead Light Railway (*see p 150*)

PUXTON AND WORLE

OPENED: 14th June 1841 (with the opening of the Bristol - Bridgwater section of the Bristol & Exeter Railway).
CLOSED: Passengers - 6th April 1964.
Goods - 10th June 1963.

Sited in the small settlement of St George's, it was an original station on the B & E Railway when it opened its first section between Bristol and Bridgwater. The village of Puxton is some two miles to the east and Worle one mile to the west. The station had a number of name changes in its early

Puxton and Worle. Looking towards Bristol from the level crossing. The principal building is on the down platform (right), with the station master's house beyond. The later wooden shelter and original small shelter behind stand on the up side.

years: opening as Banwell (another village even further away at two and a half miles to the south east) it was renamed Worle on 3rd August 1869. Renaming to Puxton came on 1st March 1884 (when another station named Worle opened on the Weston-super-Mare loop line) and then finally Puxton and Worle on 1st March 1922 (when Worle Station on the loop line closed!).

The station buildings were sited immediately east of a level crossing in St George's, the principal building being sited on the down platform. With a rather squat slate roof, two chimneys, and a canopy over the platform, it incorporated the main waiting facilities and booking office. Behind the east end of the platform stood the station master's house. From an early date a shelter with a small awning stood on the up platform; this was later supplemented by a second shelter incorporating a canopy with a fretted valence.

In addition to passengers from the surrounding rural area, Puxton and Worle Station saw major movements of milk traffic. An early photograph illustrates staff 'ready for the milk train'. Other photos show a large number of churns on the platform.

A large signal box was sited to the west of the level crossing on the down side; this is still in place though supported by wooden bracing. Apart from some sections of original gates and railings, no trace of the station remains at track side east of the now automated level crossing. The former station master's house continues in residential use.

Pylle. The attractive station building adjacent to the A37 road bridge.

PYLLE

OPENED: 3rd February 1862 (with the opening of the Glastonbury - Cole section of the Somerset Central Railway).

CLOSED: Passengers - 7th March 1966 (with closure of the Evercreech Junction - Highbridge line to passenger traffic).

Goods - 10th June 1963.

Opening with the line in 1862, the station was sited west of, and adjacent to, the A37 (Fosse Way). It was about a mile north east of Pylle village and, at an altitude of 275 ft, was nearly at the highest point of the Highbridge to Evercreech Junction line. The attractive small stone station building was on the eastern end of the up (south) side platform. With two tall chimneys but no canopy, it incorporated the station's main waiting room and booking office. Only a small wooden shelter was provided on the down platform on which also stood a section of the large stone goods shed served by a siding behind the platform. Very unusually a station master's house was directly attached to the east end of the goods shed facing the A37. Also at the east of this platform was a milk loading platform partly under the A37

road bridge. Inter-platform pedestrian movements were via wooden boards near the bridge.

A little way west of the station on the up side were cattle pens , whilst Pylle signal box stood at the west end of the up platform. This closed on 8th December 1929 at the same time as the station passing loop was lifted, thus eliminating access by trains to the down platform and milk loading dock. The down side shelter was then demolished. The siding to the goods shed remained in place controlled by a ground frame at the old signal box. The goods siding closed on 10th June 1963 and the box was demolished two years later. Staffing ceased on 4th November 1957 and Pylle was reduced in status to a halt.

After station closure in 1966, the former goods shed was used as a meat packing plant with an extension partly covering the old track bed. A period followed when the shed was disused but in the late 1980s it was developed into a large residence. The station master's house had continued in residential use and the former station building itself has also now been converted into a house. Overall the station site has been changed into a significant residential complex incorporating both conversions and new development. Some sections of the old up platform remain but the old A37 road bridge to the east has been demolished, replaced by an embankment.

RADFORD AND TIMSBURY HALT

OPENED: 9th May 1910 (with the opening of the Camerton - Limpley Stoke line).

CLOSED: 21st September 1925 (with closure of the Hallatrow - Limpley Stoke line to passenger traffic). Temporary closure 22nd March 1915 - 9th July 1923, originally as a war time measure.

Shortly after construction of the Camerton to Limpley Stoke line had commenced, it was decided that the service over the whole line including the earlier Hallatrow - Camerton section would be worked by steam rail-motor cars. The intention was to construct a series of halts, including one to serve the villages of Radford and Timsbury, the latter some one mile to the north. The platform, 150 ft long and 8 ft wide, was constructed of timber baulks. A corrugated iron waiting shelter of the pagoda type, much used by the GWR at this time, was provided together with a nameboard, wooden fencing and oil lighting. Access to the halt was via a path down from the south side of the adjacent road bridge.

Today two posts of old railway track probably mark where the access path left the road, south of the road bridge, and a short section of low wall north of the station site can be seen.

Above right Radford and Timsbury Halt. A train arrives from Limpley Stoke via Camerton shortly after the halt opened to passengers in 1910.

Below Radstock North. A view west of this attractive station with typical S & D features. Note the level crossing gates, a continuing feature for many years.

RADSTOCK

For many years Radstock was the centre of the North Somerset Coalfield. Activities associated with the collieries dominated the town and the railways played a key role. The tracks of two railway companies crossed just to the west of the town centre, the Bristol & North Somerset Railway from Bristol to Radstock and the S & D's Bath Green Park to Evercreech Junction and Poole. The two Radstock stations opening in 1873 and 1874 were right in the town centre just east of the north to south A367 road. The resulting two level crossings, yards from each other, caused major road congestion for years.

RADSTOCK NORTH

OPENED: 20th July 1874 (with the opening of the Bath extension of the Somerset & Dorset Railway from Evercreech Junction to Bath).

CLOSED: Passengers - 7th March 1966 (with closure of the Bath Green Park - Poole line to passenger traffic).

Goods - 15th June 1964 (except private sidings).

Sited just to the north of the Bristol and North Somerset Station and adjacent to the Market House, this was another very typical S & D small station. The suffix 'North' was formally added on 26th September 1949. On the up platform was the main building with two chimneys but in this case with an upward sloping canopy (a contrast to Midsomer Norton South). This building included a separate waiting room for ladies as well as the general waiting room and a booking office. Other buildings contained the gentlemen's toilets and accommodation for the station master and porters. The down platform was provided with a small wooden shelter and there was a large signal box beyond the end of the platform adjacent to the level crossing. An open footbridge at the east end gave inter-platform access but this was demolished in the 1950s before the station closed. The downside shelter was demolished in mid 1967 and the main station buildings in 1979/80.

An extensive goods yard was sited to the east of the station with goods shed, cattle pens and cranes. Much of the activity in this busy yard was associated with the local collieries.

Today a housing development covers the goods yard. The station site itself is now a landscaped car park, at the west end of which a former colliery wheel commemorates the town's industrial past.

RADSTOCK WEST

OPENED: 3rd September 1873 (with the opening of the Bristol & North Somerset Railway from Bristol to Radstock).

CLOSED: Passengers - 2nd November 1959 (with closure of the Bristol - Radstock - Frome line to passenger traffic).

Goods - 29th November 1965.

To the south of the S & D station, Radstock West had opened ten months earlier. It opened as Radstock but was renamed Radstock West on 26th September 1949. As with the S & D station, it was a classic example of its company's architecture with the principal buildings, containing the waiting room and booking office on the up side (towards Bristol) featuring three tall chimneys and a large horizontal fretted canopy. Smaller buildings on the platform included the gentlemen's toilets and storage facilities. A typical small wooden shelter with canopy was sited on the down platform. The original signal box at the west end of the down platform was a tall wooden structure but this was later rebuilt and reduced in height.

Radstock West. A view west through the GWR station featuring the William Clarke design building on the up platform. On the down platform stands a wooden shelter and later signal box.

The main station buildings on the up side were demolished in 1963 and the site redeveloped for shopping units. The tracks through the station survived for some years as did the shelter on the down platform. The only surviving remnant, apart from a number of former station railings, is the derelict down platform isolated in an area described by a large notice as 'Radstock Regeneration Site'.

ROADWATER

West Somerset Mineral Railway (*see p 157)*

SALTFORD

OPENED: 16th December 1840 (on the Bristol Temple Meads - Bath Spa section of the GWR Bristol - London line originally opened through this site some four months earlier).

CLOSED: Passengers - 5th January 1970.
Goods - 1st September 1959.

Saltford opened soon after trains began operating on the Bristol to Bath GWR line. The main buildings were always sited on the down platform nearest Saltford High Street. The original timber structure was burnt down in August 1873 and was replaced by a stone structure which then served throughout the life of the station. The up platform housed a small wooden shelter and an open footbridge connected the two platforms. A long prominent footbridge over

Saltford. An early view towards Saltford tunnel and Bristol before the eastwards extension of the platform in 1909.

the line west of the station towards Saltford tunnel was not provided by the GWR but an access path from the up side platform led to the bridge. In spring 1951 timber extensions to the platform which had been added in June 1909 were replaced by brick and pre-cast concrete slabs.

A small goods yard with a small signal box on the down side did not come into operation until November 1909. The single siding mainly dealt with coal and agricultural products, often from the Newton Park estate west of Bath.

Through the years passengers came to Saltford Station for the regatta held on the nearby River Avon. Bath race course also generated traffic, though from the station it was at least a two and a half mile walk 700 ft up hill via a ferry over the river.

Today the station and platform have disappeared. Part of a wooden kissing gate that gave access to the station remains on the down side at the Bristol end. Much of the site is in use by railway contractors, in spring 2002 work was being undertaken to stabilise the deep cutting west of the former station site. Plans have been put forward for the reopening of Saltford Station but difficult access onto the busy A4 may prove an obstacle.

SANDFORD AND BANWELL

OPENED: 3rd August 1869 (with the opening of the
Yatton - Cheddar section of the Cheddar Valley &
Yatton Railway).

CLOSED: Passengers - 9th September 1963 (with closure
of the Yatton - Witham line to passenger traffic).
Goods - 10th June 1963.

Serving the villages of Sandford to the east and
Banwell to the west, the station was sited on a north-
south section of the Cheddar Valley line just south of
the A368. When opened, only the name Sandford
was used but 'and Banwell' was soon added. The
platform and station buildings were sited to the east
of the line and were almost identical to those at
Congresbury, the next station to the north. The main
building with decorative tiles, cruciform ridge tiles,
B & E barge boards and small canopy included the
general waiting room, booking office and ladies'
waiting room and toilet. The gent's toilet had a
separate entrance adjacent to the gate which gave
access to the platform and station buildings. A stone
built store, with decorative barge boards, stood at
the south end of the platform. No second platform
was ever constructed.

A large through road goods shed, about twice the
size of the main station building, stood to the south.
The goods yard covered an area behind the station
buildings and goods shed. Cattle pens were also
provided. On 12th December 1905 a crossing loop
came into operation and a new signal box opened on
the up side, some distance south of the station. A
station master's house was provided, south east of
the station and goods yard.

Shapwick. Action on 6th April 1959 with a token
exchange for a train to Highbridge. The wooden building
dates from 1900.

Sandford and Banwell. A pre-1905 view south before the
crossing loop and signal box were constructed. The fine
B & E building and goods shed survive today, used by
Sandford Stone.

Like its twin station, Congresbury, to the north,
Sandford and Banwell never saw great volumes of
passenger traffic; the number of tickets issued in
1903 of 14,514, gradually fell to 10,679 in 1923 and
then more dramatically to 3,941 in 1933.

Following closure of the station in 1963, the
buildings remained largely intact and in the late
1970s were taken over and restored by Sandford
Stone. Visitors to the site today can see sections of
the former platform, the main stone building and
adjacent store, complete with barge boards, roof and
ridge tiles, and the former goods shed. Altogether, it
is one of the best preserved examples of a B & E
station complex in Somerset and well worth a visit.
The former station master's house is in use for
storage purposes.

SHAPWICK

OPENED: 28th August 1854 (with the opening of the
Highbridge Wharf - Glastonbury section of the
Somerset Central Railway).

CLOSED: Passengers - 7th March 1966 (with closure of
the Evercreech Junction - Highbridge line to
passenger traffic).
Goods - 10th June 1963.

Situated in a remote area on the Somerset Levels,
some two and a half miles north of the village it
served, the station opened with the line in August

Shepton Mallet Charlton Road. Looking north towards Radstock and Bath at the S & D station.

1854. The distance from Shapwick itself was reflected in the inclusion of 'Shapwick Road' Station on early maps! A long crossing loop was sited at this point on the line. Earth and timber platforms originally served the two tracks but these were replaced in the 1930s by Southern Railway type concrete components.

The up platform (towards Highbridge) was, for most of its life, provided with a wooden building with general and ladies' waiting rooms and a booking office. This replaced an earlier building which was burnt down on 25th September 1900. A small parcels office also stood on the up platform. Originally a small wooden shelter stood on the down side platform but this was not replaced when the platforms were rebuilt.

South east of the level crossing at the east of the station was a small goods yard with cattle pens and a private goods shed. During the early twentieth century, peat traffic was a major source of revenue but much of this traffic was later lost to road haulage. A signal box controlling the level crossing stood east of the crossing on the down (north) side and to the north of the box was a large house, built in 1861, with accommodation for the station master and signalman.

The only remnant of the station site today is a solitary concrete post at the entrance to the former goods yard; Station Farm is a little to the north and all around is evidence of the peat working which once provided business for the railway.

SHEPTON MALLET CHARLTON ROAD

OPENED: 20th July 1874 (with the opening of the Bath extension of the Somerset & Dorset Railway from Evercreech Junction to Bath).

CLOSED: Passengers - 7th March 1966 (with closure of the Bath Green Park - Poole line to passenger traffic).

Goods - 10th June 1963.

The S & D station was nearly a mile to the east of the town centre. The suffix 'Charlton Road' appears to have been used from the early date of October 1883. The main stone built buildings, on the up platform on the town side of the station, included waiting rooms for general use and for ladies, a booking hall and office, the station master's office and toilet facilities. An angled canopy, typical of stations on the S & D, was a feature, a shelter screen being provided at the southern end of the platform. A separate small wooden parcels office was a later addition alongside and south of the main building.

The down side platform had a small stone built waiting shelter with canopy, a gent's urinal and an attractive S & D design signal box to which a small balcony was later added. Behind the platform was a large water tower on a stone built base. For some years an unusual solid-sided open footbridge connected the platforms in a central position; this was later replaced by an open lattice structure. A large station master's house stood on Charlton Road just east of the station.

The station had extensive goods facilities, with a large goods shed, together with a cattle dock, on the

up side at the Evercreech end. On the down side, behind and to the north east of the station, stone handling and crushing machinery served local quarries.

The station itself was demolished over the period 1970 to 1972 and completely cleared for redevelopment in 1972. Today there is virtually no evidence that the station and railway ever existed in the area, apart from the embankment end on Charlton Road. The whole area is now covered by industrial and commercial development, the station site itself being largely occupied by a haulage contractor.

SHEPTON MALLET HIGH STREET

OPENED: 9th November 1858 (with the opening of the Witham - Shepton Mallet section of the East Somerset Railway).

CLOSED: Passengers - 9th September 1963 (with closure of the Yatton - Witham line to passengers).
Goods - 13th July 1964.

Shepton Mallet (the suffix 'High Street' was not added until 26th September 1949) acted as the western terminus of the East Somerset Railway from November 1858 until its extension to Wells in March 1861. The station was sited conveniently at the southern end of the High Street, in contrast with the S & D station which was nearly a mile to the east of the town centre. For over thirty five years there was only one platform and a stone building, with canopy and tall chimneys, on the north side of the line. On 8th January 1895 the south side platform came into use, with a brick built shelter with small canopy. This

Shepton Mallet High Street. Looking east towards the road bridge, the main buildings to the left close to the southern end of the High Street.

was, in effect, an island platform, a loop line serving the cattle pens behind. A large footbridge with a pitched roof connected the platforms. As with many stations on this line south of the Mendips, passenger traffic dropped markedly between 1903 and 1933 with the number of tickets issued falling from 29,631 to 6,308.

When the line was extended to Wells, a small engine shed, west of the station on the town side, was enlarged and became the main goods shed. A variety of freight traffic was handled but it was mainly agricultural. Goods traffic ceased in 1964 but stone from Dulcote Quarry continued to pass through until October 1969.

Today, nearly 40 years after passenger and goods services ceased, the whole station site is in use as an industrial estate. The main station building survives, without the canopy, occupied by Mid Somerset Cleaning Supplies. The goods shed has gone.

SHOSCOMBE AND SINGLE HILL HALT

OPENED: 23rd September 1929 (on the Bath extension of the Somerset & Dorset Railway originally opened though this site in 1874).

CLOSED: 7th March 1966 (with closure of the Bath Green Park - Poole line to passenger traffic).

The halt was sited in the steep sided valley of the Wellow Brook south east of Shoscombe in the small settlement of Single Hill. It was the last passenger

Shoscombe and Single Hill Halt. The concrete
component platforms looking east on 18th May 1963.
The small booking office and waiting room are to the left
on the path to the halt.

facility provided on the Bath extension of the S & D.
Two platforms were constructed of concrete
components of the then Southern Railway pattern.
No shelters were provided on the platforms but
illumination came from ornate oil lamps. A small
booking office and waiting room stood beside the
footpath leading to the platform from the north side.
The halt was, over a period of years, looked after by
the local Chivers family and also by two sisters who
ran the ticket office. Another pedestrian access led
from the road south of the adjacent road bridge.

The halt has been completely demolished though
the abutments of the road bridge just to the east are
a clear indication of where the line passed through
the remote valley. An isolated iron post at the road
side marks the original pedestrian access to the south
side platform.

SOMERTON (SOMERSET)

OPENED: 2nd July 1906 (on the Curry Rivel - Somerton
section of the GWR cut off route Castle Cary to
Cogland Junction originally opened to this site on
12th February 1906 for freight traffic to and from
the west only).

CLOSED: Passengers - 10th September 1962 (with
withdrawal of local passenger services between
Castle Cary and Taunton).
Goods - 6th July 1964.

Somerton Station (the suffix 'Somerset' avoided
confusion with Somerton in Oxfordshire) was sited
on a curve in a cutting close to the centre of the town
and was thus well placed for residents using the local
rail motor service between Taunton and Castle Cary.
The construction of the cutting resulted in several
houses in the town being demolished. Its structures
were typical of those on the GWR cut off route and
comprised the main buildings on the up line platform
with waiting rooms, booking office and toilets and a

Somerton (Somerset). A view west towards Taunton.
The buildings are similar to others on the GWR
cut off route (eg Langport East and Charlton
Mackrell).

brick built shelter and toilets on the down platform. A covered footbridge stood at the Taunton (west) end of the station. A goods shed was sited on a siding at the Taunton end of the up side adjacent to the cattle market. A 1906 signal box stood at the end of the platform on the down side. A new box, installed in December 1942, operated the up and down loops which were in use west of the station from summer 1943 until December 1960.

The initial seven staff increased to nine in the 1930s. The passenger tickets issued ranged from 12,207 in 1913 to 7,210 in 1933.

Today only small sections of railway fencing along the down side approach road, Station Path, remain. However plans have been put forward to reinstate rail services to this expanding Somerset town.

SPARKFORD

OPENED: 1st September 1856 (with the opening of the Frome - Yeovil section of the Wilts, Somerset & Weymouth Railway).

CLOSED: Passengers - 3rd October 1966.
Goods - 7th January 1963.

The station, on the northern edge of the village, opened at one of a number of passing places on the then single track broad gauge line from Castle Cary to Yeovil. After conversion to standard gauge in 1874, Sparkford remained a passing place until doubling of the line in 1881.

The station consisted of two platforms with the main stone buildings with canopy on the up platform (towards Castle Cary). As with many Wilts, Somerset & Weymouth stations a cast iron gent's urinal was also on the platform, at the Yeovil end. A large stone built waiting shelter, with a small canopy, stood on the down platform. No footbridge was ever

Sparkford. Looking north from the old A303 road bridge on 1st October 1966.

provided. A signal box, opened in May 1887, was sited off the down platform at the Castle Cary end. Passenger numbers reduced significantly between 1903 and 1933 with the number of passenger tickets issued falling from 12,677 to 4,239.

A large former broad gauge goods shed, together with a dock siding, cattle pens and coal wharves stood on the up side of the station also at the Castle Cary end. Freight traffic at Sparkford included coal for Messrs Perrys and later Messrs Snows, large tree trunks, arriving on flat trucks for Raymond's Sawmills, agricultural machinery and cattle feed. The designated siding for Raymond's Sawmills was again to the north of the station but this time on the down side. War Department sidings were also added from 20th May 1944. Milk was another important commodity. To the south west of the station, beyond the A303 road bridge on the up side, was a large creamery, originally owned by the Sparkford Vale Co-op Dairy Company and later United Dairies. From two sidings, added in 1932, rail milk tankers were despatched to London Kensington Olympia.

The sidings to the north of the station were taken out of use on 11th February 1962 and the station itself closed to goods traffic in January 1963. The milk sidings ceased operation on 12th December 1963 and the signal box closed as from 30th November 1966. The station closed for passenger traffic in October 1966. No line side remains can be seen.

The line, singled with the removal of the up line in May 1968, is now crossed north of the former station site by the A303 Sparkford By-pass. The former creamery is occupied by Haynes Publishing, famous for publication of Haynes Car Manuals.

STOGUMBER

OPENED: 31st March 1862 (with the opening of the West Somerset Railway from Norton Junction to Watchet).

CLOSED: Passengers - 4th January 1971 (with closure of the Norton Fitzwarren - Minehead line).
Goods - 19th August 1963.

REOPENED: 7th May 1978 (with the reopening of the Williton - Stogumber section of the restored West Somerset Railway).

The station layout is unique on the Minehead line with the platform and main building on opposite sides of the track, the station building on the north east side and the platform on the south west. The platform was built in three sections. The original stone section was extended towards Taunton in the early 1900s using old sleepers and in 1933 it was extended again, this time towards Minehead using sleepers with concrete supports. A wooden shelter was installed at the southern end of the platform. For some time a small signal box stood on the platform but this closed on 6th April 1926. Access to the platform was via footboards across the line at the Bishops Lydeard end. There was no mains water at the site and water was pumped from a well to a tank in the station building roof. A station master's house was built to the north of the station above the approach road.

A goods loop was provided on the north east side to serve a large goods shed at the Minehead end of the site. A further siding at the Taunton end, accessed via points in front of the station, served a loading dock and shed and cattle pens. For many years a camping coach was sited in this goods loading

Above left Stogumber. The isolated station building (left) and the wooden platform with wooden shelter (right) on 30th October 1965.

Above Strap Lane halt. Looking south towards Bruton in the late 1940s. Two small wooden huts provide limited shelter at this isolated halt.

siding. Use of the goods shed ceased on 19th August 1963 and it was demolished the same year.

The attractive station building and other facilities remained largely unchanged for many years but Stogumber became unstaffed as from 26th February 1968 until its closure in 1971. Following its reopening by the West Somerset Railway, considerable work was undertaken to the platform, the wooden sections of which had deteriorated. In 1992 a new wooden shelter made by local craftsmen was erected and, for a time, the earlier shelter was isolated with a section of the platform out of use. Today both shelters are in use, but a section of the platform at the Minehead end is currently out of use pending refurbishment of the timber part of the platform.

From 1948 the former station master's house was the home of Harry Horn who acted as Stogumber station master for part of the West Somerset Railway era until his death in 2000 aged 96. During British Rail days he was signalman at both Bishops Lydeard and Williton. In his memory a roofed picnic table and bench has been installed in the well tended picnic area laid out on the site of the former goods shed. Early in 2001 nine period style lamps were erected on the platform, on the former station building and in the car parking area to further enhance this beautiful small station.

STRAP LANE HALT

OPENED: 18th July 1932 (on the Frome - Yeovil section of the Wilts, Somerset & Weymouth Railway originally opened through this site in 1856).

CLOSED: 5th June 1950.
Temporary closure 6th October 1941 - 16th December 1946 as a war time measure.

Strap Lane Halt was one of the fourteen halts and platforms constructed by the GWR in 1932. The halt on the two track main GWR line to the West Country, a little north of Bruton, comprised two timber platforms with small wooden shelters. The halt was principally served by auto trains on the Westbury to Taunton services. It closed completely in 1950 and today no trace of the halt remains.

SUTTON BINGHAM

OPENED: 19th July 1860 (with the opening of the Yeovil Junction - Exeter section of the London & South Western Railway).

CLOSED: Passengers - 31st December 1962.
Goods: - 4th April 1960.

Sited about half a mile north of Sutton Bingham itself and a mile south of East Coker, the station was different architecturally from others on the Yeovil to Exeter line (eg Crewkerne). Featuring four tall chimneys, the main building on the up north side housed the main offices and accommodation for the station master. A horizontal canopy covered a section of the platform. A wooden shelter with a canopy served passengers on the down line; no footbridge was ever provided, connections being via Sutton Bingham. A train towards Yeovil approaches the up platform at this relatively little used station close to the Dorset border.

footboards at the east end of the station. A small signal box stood at the Yeovil end of the down platform and a small goods yard with three short sidings was sited on the up side, also at the Yeovil end. In all it was a relatively well equipped station considering the low level of traffic in this rural area.

By the mid 1950s the canopies had been removed from both buildings and Sutton Bingham was downgraded to a staffed halt on 1st August 1960. It closed just over two years later: the final timetable showed six down and five up trains per day, weekdays only. The goods yard had closed earlier, in 1960. The signal box remained in operation until 14th February 1965. Today a small section of the face of the original up side platform can be seen, all that remains of this little used station.

TAUNTON

OPENED: 1st July 1842 (with the opening of the Bridgwater - Taunton section of the Bristol & Exeter Railway).

CLOSED: Passengers - remains open for services on the Bristol - Taunton - Exeter and London - Taunton - Exeter lines).
Goods - 1965

Opening in July 1842 as the terminus of the second section of the B & E Railway from Bridgwater, Taunton commenced its role as the most important centre in Somerset for passenger and freight traffic.

Taunton. The downside exterior in about 1905. The two storey building is a survivor of the original 1842 station.

Following these direct links with Bristol and London, a further main line extension to the West Country through Exeter opened in 1844. In the following thirty years, Taunton also became a focus of radiating branch lines to Yeovil (1853), Watchet (1862)/Minehead (1874), Chard (1866) and Wiveliscombe (1871)/Barnstaple (1873).

With the town at that time lying principally to the south of the new railway, the first 1842 station was built to Brunel's 'one sided' design (also used originally at Exeter, Reading and Slough). Two separate stations were built on the same side of the main line, that at the east end being used by up trains to London and that at the west end used by down trains to Exeter. Between the platforms of the two stations, the tracks crossed each other; they also crossed at the London end to ease the complicated movements. The two stations each had their own buildings with roofs extending over the tracks; the up station being single storey and the down two storey. With both stations on the town side of the railway, passengers did not have to cross the tracks but operationally it was difficult and some considered it dangerous. A carriage shed was sited opposite the down platform and opposite the up platform stood the original goods shed. Outside the two stations, across the forecourt, 'The Great Western Hotel' was built to serve rail passengers.

Major increases in traffic made it essential for a more conventional layout to be adopted. The 1842 down platform was lengthened and the down building adapted; the old up platform and building were demolished and a new up platform and building were erected on the other side of the tracks. An overall roof was added, the changes being completed on 17th August 1868. A contemporary account described the new down side building: 'Wings of offices and waiting and refreshment rooms extend on either side of the old (1842) square block of building, the elevation of which is embellished by a glazed veranda'. The new roof was 200 ft long and 88 ft wide and from the braces and ties supporting the roof hung some fifty globe shaped lamps. The 1868 down platform was 21 ft wide and 540 ft long - 250 ft within the main station walls, 60 ft outside towards Bristol and 230 ft over Station Road bridge towards Wellington. The up platform was wider at 28 ft 6 inches but was shorter - at the western end it extended only 33 ft beyond the wall as far as Station Road and 60 ft beyond the wall at the Bristol end.

The three tracks between the platforms were spanned underneath the roof by an iron bridge some 7½ ft wide. On both the up and down platforms were waiting rooms (both general and for ladies only) and booking offices. The superintendent's office, parcels office and refreshment rooms were on the down side. In 1895 the platforms were further extended, that on the up side taking in the old goods shed site; Taunton now had the longest platforms on the GWR. Bay platforms were added at each end of the main platforms to deal with the terminating trains from all the branch lines which by that time were focusing on the station. These extensions and bays were provided with canopies on columns.

By the end of the nineteenth century the development of Taunton as a major rail centre led to serious congestion. To ease the situation a goods

Taunton. A view from the east in about 1905, showing the overall roof in place from 1868, until major changes associated with quadrupling of the tracks in 1931/1932.

avoiding loop line was constructed south of the station in 1896. This loop was built approximately on the line of the old Grand Western Canal which had been bought by the B & E in 1864 and then closed in this section through Taunton. The loop included a new bridge over Station Road replacing a former canal aqueduct. A goods shed was built alongside the loop south-east of the station replacing that previously lost through the extensions of the up platform. The first locomotive shed at Taunton was a small two road temporary timber building first erected at Bridgwater, then dismantled and re-erected at Taunton when the line was extended there in 1842. In 1860 it was re-sited again nearer the passenger station to allow track alterations. It was then closed in April 1896 and replaced by a large brick built shed west of Station Road off the newly opened avoiding line. Costing some £10,500, it had twenty eight radiating 'roads' or tracks.

Ad hoc improvements and changes to both the track layout and station buildings took place between 1896 and 1930 but the next major re-building of Taunton Station came with the quadrupling of the tracks between Cogland Junction east of Taunton and Norton Fitzwarren to the west. This started in September 1930 and was finished in April 1932. The 1878 overall roof was demolished and a new layout of four through platform faces (two on a new island platform) and five bay platforms was brought into use. The buildings on the down side, including the original two storey 1842 block, were largely retained but re-building took place on the up side. The length of the through platforms ranged from 1200 ft - 1400 ft; the bay platforms continued, as in 1895, at each end of the two outer platforms now with an extra bay at the west end of the down platform to accommodate trains to both Minehead and Barnstaple. The footbridge was replaced by a subway 140 ft long and 15 ft wide coming into use on 17th January 1932. The unusual bronze hoods over the lamps at the foot of the stairs on either side are still in place. A new entrance and booking office with elaborate glazed tiles was built at the north end of the new subway. The major re-modelling of the station had generally been completed by December 1931. The island platform served most long distance trains; facilities such as refreshment rooms and bookstalls were provided on the outer platforms.

Once upgrading of the passenger station had been completed, work started on improving the goods facilities. The relatively small brick goods shed on the down side of the 1896 goods avoiding line was demolished and a new brick built goods shed, almost double the size of the old, opened on 20th February 1932. A flat roofed warehouse was also built at the east end. A two storey goods depot and office was also opened on Canal Road on the south side of the goods yard. With these improved facilities, Taunton became a major focus for freight traffic in the West Country; inward traffic was dominated by coal, serving businesses over a wide area in and around Taunton. Outward traffic was of a wide variety but largely associated with agriculture, cattle movements

being particularly important with the goods yard very close to the busy Taunton Livestock Market.

In 1963 Taunton was designated a Freight Concentration Depot, but road haulage eventually took its toll on the extensive goods facilities, the impact being especially hard because of the proximity of the M5 motorway. The goods yard and the avoiding line closed in 1965 and the Freight Concentration Depot in 1972. The large number of railway owned road vehicles based at the station that had for many years delivered goods over a wide area of Somerset, were no longer to be seen.

The development and changes to the signalling around Taunton Station was particularly complicated; a number of small boxes were eventually replaced by five boxes following the 1930s quadrupling. The boxes were closed over the period 1963 to 1987 due to a combination of track closures and rationalisation and finally, the building and commissioning of the Exeter power box which now controls all signalling in the Taunton area.

Both passenger and freight traffic was heavy during and after the Second World War (on summer Saturdays in 1957 up to 170 express trains stopped at or passed through the station) but, as with freight, passenger traffic at Taunton began to dwindle in the 1960s, particularly with the withdrawal of services on all the branch lines focusing on the station. The two faces of the island platform were taken out of use in March 1967, the two central lines being then

Taunton. The island platform looking down post 1931. Now re-opened following a long period of disuse.

used only by through passenger and freight trains. The building and canopies were removed and replaced on the retained platform by trees and advertisement hoardings.

On 16th March 1983 a new booking office and travel centre was opened on the north side. This completely reversed the original 1840s arrangements, with the main reception and booking facilities now only on the up side. Today, Taunton is a busy station with inter-city trains to London, the Midlands and the West Country and local trains on the Bristol to Exeter line. A major change came in 2000 with the re-instatement of the island platform for use by both inter-city and local trains. The old entrance from the subway has been renovated and a new platform shelter erected. Once again Taunton Station has four through platform faces in use, together with a bay at the north end of the up platform, used occasionally for local trains in the Bristol direction.

The former goods shed and offices are still used, the latter with the title 'G.W. Goods Offices' still clearly to be seen. The former Railway Hotel is now offices named 'Great Western House'. The white lettering 'British Railways Taunton Freight Concentration Depot' on a derelict building on the down side, east of the station, is a relic of times past.

TEMPLECOMBE

Located in the heart of rural Somerset, Templecombe played a key role in the railway life of this part of southern England at the crossing point of the London & South Western Railway main London to Plymouth route and the north-south S & D line from Bath to the south coast. This account covers the history of three stations/platforms at Templecombe.

The first station, later known as Templecombe Upper, opened in May 1860 with the completion of the section of the Salisbury & Yeovil Railway from Gillingham to Sherborne. The second station, later known as Templecombe Lower, opened in February 1862, some half mile north east of the first as the southern terminus of the Cole to Templecombe section of the Dorset Central Railway. At the same time the Glastonbury to Cole section of the Somerset Central Railway opened. Following amalgamation of the Dorset Central and Somerset Central Railways as the S & D Railway, a further section southwards from Templecombe Lower opened in September 1863 thus completing the through route from the Bristol Channel at Burnham-on-Sea to the English Channel at Poole.

Templecombe, now at a major railway cross roads, saw considerable interchange of passengers and goods over the years. From an early date links were made between the east-west and north-south routes.

Templecombe Lower. The original Dorset Central Station closed in 1887 and subsequently used in the S & D goods yard.

From March 1870, a spur line led south west from the S & D line, north of Templecombe, into Templecombe Upper. North-south trains now stopped there regularly, though all movements required a reversing manoeuvre into the newly provided bay platform on the north side of Templecombe Upper.

In January 1887 Templecombe Lower closed, becoming for many years a major goods yard for the S & D, and on the same date a small Lower Platform was opened south of Templecombe Lower and immediately north of the actual crossing point of the two lines. The Platform was used by the occasional S & D train that did not go into Templecombe Upper. This latter station now became a major focus of activity, in particular with its siting approximately half way between London and Plymouth: the London & South Western Railway boat trains exchanged engines at Templecombe.

TEMPLECOMBE LOWER

OPENED: 3rd February 1862 (with the opening of the Cole - Templecombe section of the Dorset Central Railway).

CLOSED: 17th January 1887 (following the diversion of most through Somerset & Dorset passenger trains to Templecombe Upper on the Salisbury - Yeovil line).

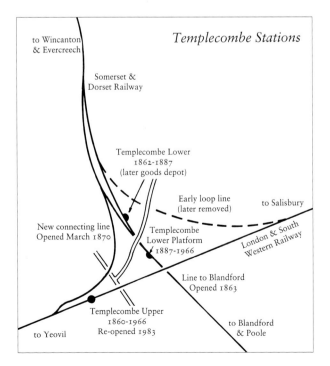

Templecombe Stations

to Wincanton & Evercreech

Somerset & Dorset Railway

Templecombe Lower 1862-1887 (later goods depot)

Early loop line (later removed)

to Salisbury

New connecting line Opened March 1870

Templecombe Lower Platform 1887-1966

London & South Western Railway

Line to Blandford Opened 1863

to Yeovil

Templecombe Upper 1860-1966 Re-opened 1983

to Blandford & Poole

Above Templecombe Upper. Much activity at the station on the up island platform. Note the magnificent canopy, replaced during the 1930s.

Left Templecombe Lower Platform. A view on 29th July 1962 of the little used 1887 platform. The main London & South Western Railway line is on the embankment beyond the platform.

TEMPLECOMBE LOWER PLATFORM

OPENED: 17th January 1887 (replacing the earlier Templecombe Lower Station a little to the north; the Platform serving trains not calling at Templecombe Upper).

CLOSED: 3rd January 1966.

TEMPLECOMBE UPPER

OPENED: 7th May 1860 (with the opening of the Gillingham - Sherborne section of the Salisbury & Yeovil Railway operated by the London & South Western Railway).

CLOSED: Passengers - 7th March 1966 (with closure of the Bath Green Park - Poole line to passenger traffic). Goods - 5th April 1965.

REOPENED: 3rd October 1983 (serving trains on the Salisbury - Yeovil - Exeter line).

Facilities at Templecombe Upper were extensive; the main station approach road led to the down side and for many years the link to the up (island) platform was via a subway. The station master's house was incorporated in the down side building. Both up and down platforms were covered with canopies, that on the up side had a major extension of a completely different vaulted design. These extensive canopies provided shelter to passengers exchanging between the north-south trains at the bay platform and the up trains to London. A large signal box was sited at the Yeovil end of the up platform. A major goods yard, handling a large range of freight, was developed over the years west of the station with the goods shed and cattle pens on the down side. Milk was a major commodity. The scale of operations at Templecombe Upper between the two World Wars can be judged by the following 1928 figures: passenger tickets issued, 24,136; passenger tickets collected, 28,181; milk cans forwarded, 24,902; lavatory pennies(!) collected, 12,240.

Because of all this railway activity through the years, a large proportion of the local residents were involved in some manner with railway work.

During the late 1930s the Southern Railway undertook a station rebuilding programme and, because of its importance as a junction, Templecombe was selected for major work. In 1938 the station was completely re-modelled in the Southern Railway style. Platforms were lengthened to accommodate trains of fourteen coaches; these platforms covered by large canopies stretched east to the road underbridge. The island platform on the up side was widened and a new art-deco style signal box was built at the west end. The subway was replaced by a concrete bridge.

During the Second World War, a fully equipped ambulance train on instant call out was based at the strategically placed Templecombe Station. The medical facilities on board were unfortunately needed on 5th September 1942 when three bombs brought major damage and casualties at and around the station. Unfortunately two trains had just arrived when the bombs fell causing extensive damage to the trains and station buildings. Thirteen people were killed, including five railwaymen, and many others were injured.

After the War, with the damage repaired, traffic again revived and steadily increased with many local residents travelling by train to work, to school or on holiday. The exchange function also flourished. Freight traffic did well; the Upper yard was enlarged but the former S & D Lower yard closed on 5th May 1950, continuing to be used just as a motive power depot.

By the early 1960s however, decline had set in, through Midlands to south coast traffic being diverted away from the S & D line. Goods traffic ceased in 1964 and the passenger station closed in March 1966 with the withdrawal of passenger services on the former S & D route from Bath to Poole. The little used Lower Platform had closed earlier in January 1966.

Templecombe became a depressed community with the main local employer gone and rail links to other parts of the country removed. The main station building was demolished in 1968 and much of the Salisbury to Exeter route was reduced to single track. The signal box was retained.

But this was not the end for Templecombe Station - thanks largely to the sterling efforts of the Templecombe Station Working Committee (T.S.W.C.). During the 1970s various surveys and studies had been undertaken but relatively little progress was made. The turning point came with the inaugural meeting of the T.S.W.C on 19th March

Templecombe. An up train to London Waterloo at the reopened station on 6th March 2002. Note the 1938 art-deco signal box now used in the upper storey as a ticket office.

1982. After early difficulties British Rail agreed to stop a train at Templecombe once again using the former up platform. Building on initial success the T.S.W.C organised a number of excursions from Templecombe, also undertaking a large amount of voluntary work at the station to meet the requirements of British Rail. This included the provision of lighting. The excursions were a great success and the Committee earned the respect of the County Council and British Rail. Eventually, after extensive work had been undertaken by the Committee, the station reopened on 3rd October 1983, initially for a three year experiment; half the upper floor of the signal box doubling as a booking office. In 1988 a small platform shelter was built; this was added to in 1990 by the construction of a new building with toilets and other facilities. A 1893 footbridge was also erected, transferred from the station at Buxted in East Sussex.

Through the 1990s business continued to flourish. In the 1980s and 1990s the station itself, through support of volunteers from the Templecombe Station Promotion Group, won many local and national awards as 'Best Kept Station', including (in 1995) first prize in the national award for 'Small stations in the rural and suburban category'. Well tended flower beds and a lawn enhance the station. On the lawn stands a sun dial sculpture erected in 1990, commissioned by the British Rail Community Unit and titled 'Tempus fugit'.

Thorney and Kingsbury Halt. The concrete component halt with small shelter on 17th March 1962.

Today there are regular passenger services to London (Waterloo), Salisbury and Exeter. The service is reduced from the 1950s level but for residents in south Somerset and north Dorset Templecombe is a very welcome and well used facility. In March 2002 the ticket office was open from 0600 hrs. to 2200 hrs. on weekdays and 0915 hrs. to 2045 hrs. on Sundays - unusual today at a relatively small station.

Thornfalcon. The wooden buildings on 28th April 1962: from left to right the main station building, a small parcels office and the signal box.

THORNEY AND KINGSBURY HALT

OPENED: 28th November 1927 (on the Durston - Yeovil branch originally opened through this site in 1853).

CLOSED: 15th June 1964 (with the closure of the Taunton - Yeovil line to passenger traffic).

Three miles north of Martock, the halt, made of concrete components, was under the bridge carrying the road from Kingsbury Episcopi to Muchelney. Steps from the road bridge led down to the platform which had a small shelter, and attractive oil lamps. A small office was in one end of the shelter. A siding for the Nestles milk depot on the Yeovil side of the halt was opened in November 1932.

Early in 2002 little remained to be seen of the halt; only a small part of the concrete platform could be detected north west of the road, together with a section of fencing at the top of the original footpath to the halt. The adjacent milk depot was derelict.

THORNFALCON

OPENED: 1871 (on the Taunton - Chard branch of the Bristol & Exeter Railway originally opened through this site in 1866).

CLOSED: Passengers - 10th September 1962 (with closure of the Taunton - Chard Junction line to passenger traffic).

Goods - 6th July 1964.

Temporary closure to all traffic from 3rd February to 7th May 1951 due to a fuel crisis.

Twerton-on-Avon. The station on the viaduct above Lower Bristol Road, Bath, looking east.

The station opened as Thorne Falcon, changed to Thorne until July 1890 and then to Thornfalcon as from 1st January 1902. The station buildings and platform on the west side of the single track branch line were of wooden construction, contrasting with other more imposing brick built station buildings on the branch. Some commentators state they were the least imposing on the branch but they had a style of their own blending with the local rural scene. The main buildings provided the usual facilities and there was also a small wooden parcels office with sliding doors back and front opening on to both the platform and the station yard. Oil lamps provided illumination. The original wooden platform was later replaced by concrete components. Passenger numbers were never high, numbering 542 in 1933.

Unusually a goods loop line traversed the station forecourt behind the buildings and platform. This served traders' sidings at either end. A wooden signal box, taken out of use in 1912, also stood at the north end between the platform and the forecourt. The layout generally remained unchanged from 1871 until the station closure in 1962.

Today the station site has been taken over by the northern end of the dual carriageway section of the A358 from Henlade to Ash Cross. Minor sections of railings, possibly associated with the former railway, can be seen but no traces of the station itself.

TWERTON ON AVON

OPENED: 16th December 1840 (on the Bristol Temple Meads - Bath Spa section of the GWR Bristol to London line opened through this site some four months earlier).
CLOSED: 2nd April 1917.

Sited at the eastern end of the major Twerton

viaduct, Twerton opened soon after the Bristol - Bath line was completed. Built on the site of a GWR office used during the construction of the line, it is a three storey building and, like the viaduct, is now Grade II listed. It incorporated residential accommodation which consisted of two kitchens at ground level, two bedrooms below track level; a sitting room at track level and an attic above. The station's two timber platforms were supported on cast iron brackets bolted to the face of the viaduct itself and the skew bridge over the road to Twerton High Street. A timber shelter stood on the down side platform and a stone built gentlemen's toilet on the up. In the early days inter platform movements were over footboards. However a footbridge was added later and remained until it was removed to Shrivenham in 1923. By 1884 a signal box was in place on the up platform immediately beyond the footbridge.

As the station's name was easily confused with Tiverton in Devon, it was renamed Twerton-on-Avon on 1st August 1899. Passenger numbers were never great and much business was lost when Bath Electric Tramways opened on the adjacent road into the city in January 1904. The station closed in April 1917 as a war time economy measure and never reopened.

Today the platforms have gone but the main station building stands prominently on the Lower Bristol Road, now in retail use.

VENN CROSS

OPENED: 1st November 1873 (with the opening of the Wiveliscombe - Barnstaple section of the Devon and Somerset Railway).
CLOSED: Passengers - 3rd October 1966 (with closure of the Norton Fitzwarren - Barnstaple line).
Goods - 30th September 1963.

Venn Cross, located in a cutting at the second highest point (666 ft above sea level) on the Barnstaple line, was immediately west of Venn Cross tunnel. At this

Venn Cross. Looking east, in about 1958, at the tunnel and the shelter on the up platform. The photographer was standing on the Somerset/Devon border!

height, and in a cutting, the station was often prone to snow blockages. The line was originally single track at this point with one platform on the down (south) side. The station building, adjoining the station master's house, was back from and above the platform on the road side. To the west was a large goods shed and the signal box (1905) on the down platform. The county border crosses the line from north to south at this point; so, while most of the station and platform were in Somerset, the west end of the platform and the goods shed were actually in Devon! The loop line on the up side, together with a second platform and shelter with canopy, were added in April 1905; both platforms and the loop were lengthened in 1937. Passenger numbers at Venn Cross were low: in 1903, 3,107 passenger tickets were issued; this had fallen to 1,405 by 1933.

Today the station building and former station master's house are in residential use; 'Station House' on a short cul-de-sac created following the re-alignment of the B3227. A number of sections of the original railings and gates are still in place. The former goods shed has been beautifully renovated into a large residence, 'The Engine House'. To the west a distant and home signal stand in a field beside the former track alignment.

WALTON-IN-GORDANO HALT
Weston, Clevedon & Portishead Light Railway (see p 150)

WALTON PARK HALT
Weston, Clevedon & Portishead Light Railway (see p 150)

WANSTROW
OPENED: 1st January 1860 (on the Witham - Shepton Mallet section of the East Somerset Railway originally opened through this site in 1858).
CLOSED: Passengers - 9th September 1963 (with closure of the Yatton - Witham line to passenger traffic). Goods - 10th June 1963.

This station, sited to the south of the village itself, was unusual in that records show it to have been paid for by local inhabitants, as the East Somerset Railway Company could not afford to build it. At first only a small, low stone building provided shelter; there was initially no platform ramp. However the building was soon extended and a ramp and lighting provided. Unstaffed until 1st April 1909, a wooden station master's office was then built on the platform and between it and the waiting shelter, a corrugated iron lamp room. A goods loop, beyond the station at the Cranmore end, holding ten wagons, was provided in January 1927 and dealt with coal, cattle food and livestock, which were held

Wanstrow. The post 1909 facilities: from left to right, the main building, an iron lamp hut and the wooden station master's office. Note the GWR seat.

in two cattle pens. The siding closed in 1963.

In its early days, and until about 1909, the Wanstrow platform was only the length of two six wheel coaches. Staff at Cranmore and Witham were required to arrange for Wanstrow passengers to sit in compartments nearest the guard and the driver ensured that the guard's van and adjoining coach drew up alongside the platform.

Today no traces can be seen at track side. Alongside a path leading from near the rail bridge over the A361 some stone-work probably indicates the foundation of the old building. Remains of the path gate can also been seen at the road side.

WASHFORD

OPENED: 16th July 1874 (with the opening of the Minehead Railway from Minehead to Watchet).

CLOSED: Passengers - 4th January 1971 (with closure of the Norton Fitzwarren - Minehead line).
Goods - 6th July 1964.

REOPENED: 28th August 1976 (with the reopening of the Blue Anchor - Williton section of the restored West Somerset Railway).

Built on the south side of the line to the west of the town, at a cost of some £940, Washford comprises a station building and small signal box on a single platform. The latter, at the Taunton end, is immediately adjacent to the access steps from the main A39 road. On the north side of the single line there was originally a goods shed, sidings and a passing loop, the last used normally only by goods trains. No platform was ever built on this up side, though the down platform was lengthened in 1934. The small signal cabin was taken out of use in August 1952 and staffing ended as from 21st February 1966. Freight traffic ceased in July 1964, the sidings were removed and the goods shed demolished.

When the line was reopened through Washford in 1976, the station site was leased by the West Somerset Railway to the Somerset & Dorset Railway Trust which over the years has transformed the site. The Trust had been unable to secure a long term site along the former S & D route. Fortunately the main station building had been kept in reasonable condition in its last British Rail days and it has now been carefully restored and fitted out in S & D style with many artefacts from former S & D stations. It is the main museum for the Trust and many archives are kept at the station. The small signal cabin has been fitted out in the manner of the former box at Midford, south of Bath.

Similarly, the goods yard has been converted to reflect the former days of the S & D. No sidings were left by British Rail and old track from Radstock and the Royal Ordnance Factory at Puriton has been

Washford. Towards Minehead in 1947. Note the small signal cabin on the platform which remains, restored in the manner of the Midford box by the Somerset and Dorset Railway Trust.

used to lay out a number of sidings. Remnants of other S & D stations described in this book can now be found in this yard. The large new building at the west end of the former yard, used for storage and restoration work, incorporates main doors from the former goods shed at Wells Priory Road; the adjacent small office building at the Minehead end also derives from Wells. The side of the building opposite the platform incorporates a cast iron window from the former bonded warehouse at Bath Green Park. Also sited in the goods yard at the Taunton end is the small former signal box from Burnham-on-Sea; this contains a display of signalling equipment. Finally, the gates at the Minehead end of the yard across the tracks to the West Somerset Railway line are the level crossing gates from Edington Junction on the former Highbridge to Glastonbury section of the S & D.

WASHFORD

West Somerset Mineral Railway (see p 157)

WATCHET

OPENED: 31st March 1862 (as the terminus of the West Somerset Railway from Norton Junction to Watchet).

CLOSED: Passengers - 4th January 1971 (with closure of the Norton Fitzwarren - Minehead line).
Goods - 6th July 1964 (except for a private siding).

REOPENED: 28th August 1976 (with the reopening of the Blue Anchor - Williton section of the restored West Somerset Railway).

Watchet Station was originally opened in 1862 as the terminus of the West Somerset Railway from Norton

Watchet. A Taunton bound train in about 1961. The large goods shed is behind the engine. Note the GWR pagoda hut providing shelter on the platform.

Junction. The station officially opened when the first passenger train left for Taunton at 0845 hrs on 31st March. It was apparently a day of great celebration in Watchet with triumphal arches, brass bands playing and a sumptuous dinner in the evening. The coming of the railway to Watchet was due largely to trade associated with the harbour. A complex of docks sidings linked to the main line at the station was completed by June 1862. These sidings led off a passing loop originally laid out as a locomotive run-round facility. A large goods shed was also built. A locomotive turntable was at one

Watchet. The 1862 original terminus building at right angles to the line on 30th October 1965, and now used by the West Somerset Railway for a booking office and shop.

Wellington. The down Cornish Riviera Express en route to Cornwall in about 1900 passing through the original station, with characteristic Brunel style buildings on both platforms.

time sited in the docks area, there being no room elsewhere; also several mini turntables to facilitate shunting, some of which was done by horses. Goods traffic at Watchet was also associated with the paper mill to the south of the town which was rail connected from 31st January 1929. Decline came when products were diverted to road transport. In the mid 1960s the rail links into the docks and the paper mill were lifted.

Watchet remained a terminus for only twelve years until the arrival from the west of the Minehead Railway, opening in 1874. The locomotives, formerly kept at Watchet, were now stored at Minehead; Watchet's engine shed became redundant, but remained rail connected until October 1882 when the new standard gauge line by-passed it. With the opening of the through line to Minehead, more traffic was generated and a signal box was built on the embankment above the platform. This height also enabled the signalman to supervise train movements in the docks area. However, the box became disused in 1926; it remained in place, used for other railway purposes until its demolition in 1956.

Because of its original terminus status, the main stone built station building is at right angles to the track facing the road. It incorporated the usual booking and waiting facilities and a ladies' room. The gent's facilities were in a separate lean-to building at the rear of the main block. Next to this block stood a stone built office, used for lamp

storage and coal, and a large GWR corrugated iron pagoda shelter used for many years as a waiting shelter and later as a store. Throughout its life in GWR/British Rail days, Watchet Station, being located in the middle of the town, was well used by local residents as well as visitors.

When the line finally closed in 1971 the goods shed and iron footbridge at the western end were sold by British Rail to the local council. The goods shed is now used as the Watchet Boat Museum. Today the reopened station building is used as a booking office and shop for the West Somerset Railway. The other remaining platform buildings are disused - the pagoda hut is boarded up. The foundations of the former signal box are being excavated. The footbridge underwent restoration in 1992. The station continues to be used by both residents and visitors and it is hoped that the new Watchet Marina, opened in July 2001, will generate good business.

WATCHET

West Somerset Mineral Railway (see p 156)

WELLINGTON

OPENED: 1st May 1843 (with the opening of the Taunton - Beam Bridge section of the Bristol & Exeter Railway).

CLOSED: Passengers - 5th October 1964.
Goods - 6th July 1964.

Wellington Station was located on the bank of the same name as the line climbs up to Whiteball Tunnel on the Somerset/Devon border. The bank was the scene of the record breaking run of the 'City of

Wellington. Looking north towards Taunton – the rebuilt station on 15th November 1932.

Truro' locomotive in 1904 with the up 'Ocean Mails Express' (recorded speed of over 100 mph). The original station on two tracks included the main offices on the down line built in the distinctive Brunel style with an all round horizontal canopy and on the up line a stone shelter with small canopy. The two platforms were connected by an covered lattice footbridge, elaborately decorated, of a type also found elsewhere in Somerset, for instance, at Keynsham. Extensive flower and shrub beds completed the scene.

By the 1880s the station had a major goods yard, including a goods shed, mainly on the down side. Facilities, including a 9 ton capacity crane, were provided for the handling of livestock, furniture and machinery. The original signal box was on the up platform but this was replaced by east and west boxes (also on the up side) before 1911. These two boxes were in turn replaced by a new box on the up platform during the 1920s.

In the 1931/2 rebuilding process the platforms were taken back and the tracks between them quadrupled, with the two platform faces now being served by loop lines. A new open footbridge connected the two platforms. The main buildings continued to be on the down side at the end of the station approach and a waiting shelter and signal box were on the up. There were no major changes to the facilities provided for goods traffic.

Early in 2002 some remains of the down platform were visible alongside a disused loop line. The old goods shed is now joined to other buildings within extensive industrial development around the old Station Approach.

WELLOW

OPENED: 20th July 1874 (with the opening of the Bath extension of the Somerset & Dorset Railway from Evercreech Junction to Bath).
CLOSED: Passengers - 7th March 1966 (with closure of the Bath Green Park - Poole line to passenger traffic).
Goods - 10th June 1963.

South west of the village centre, Wellow Station was apparently always well used, even late on, because of the inadequacy of the bus services to and from the village. The compact station building on the up (west) platform was built of grey limestone with a slate roof, two chimneys and a downward sloping canopy. It incorporated a station master's office with an attractive bay window, combined booking hall and waiting room and a ladies' room. Also on the up platform was a gentlemen's toilet, a small stone built store room and, at the north end, a small metal shed, used as a lamp room. On the opposite down platform stood a small wooden shelter with canopy. A signal box was sited a little way north of the station on the down side. Inter-platform connection was via a timber level crossing at the south end. A small goods yard was sited south west of the station on the up side; a wooden lever cabin at the south end of the up platform operated points to the goods yard.

After closure the former station building was extended and converted into a house by the architect, Peter Blake. It featured in a *Living Homes* magazine article on old stations converted into dwellings. Today, with new owners, 'Old Station House' preserves the main features of the original station building and a new extension at the south west end has been skilfully added. An attractive garden has been created on the former trackbed with a lawn on

Wellow. A view towards Bath of this small S & D station now converted as part of a larger residence.

the filled section between the platforms, both of which are still to be seen. An old station lamp post is at the west end of the down platform. The former signal box has also been converted and extended for residential use and in early 2002, the old goods yard was in use as a small landscaped public car park.

WELLS

At one time this small cathedral city had three stations all within a short distance of one another. The first line to enter Wells was the Somerset Central broad gauge track from Glastonbury, Priory Road Station opening as the terminus on 15th March 1859. Next was the East Somerset Railway from Witham on 1st March 1862, also of broad gauge track, the terminus being just to the east of Priory Road. Lastly the Cheddar Valley & Yatton Railway from Yatton was opened to Tucker Street Station on 5th April 1870. The latter two companies were absorbed by the GWR and in 1874/5 converted to standard gauge. This brought them in line with the former Somerset Central Railway from Glastonbury which had been converted when becoming part of the S & D Railway. Through running on standard gauge track was thus now possible between all the lines. As from 1st January 1878 through trains ran from the Cheddar Valley line to the former East Somerset; they used a short stretch of S & D track. This became possible after agreement between the GWR and the Somerset & Dorset Railway. The

former East Somerset Railway terminus closed and although through running from west to east was now realised, for fifty six years the trains passed through Priory Road Station without stopping. This absurd situation persisted until 1st October 1934. Two stations were then in use until 29th October 1951 when Priory Road Station closed, leaving Tucker Street as the only station serving Wells until it too closed to passengers on 9th September 1963. All this was a far cry from the early 1870s when Wells had three stations and rail links in three directions. Early in 2002 plinths with appropriate plaques were erected, marking the sites of the three Wells stations.

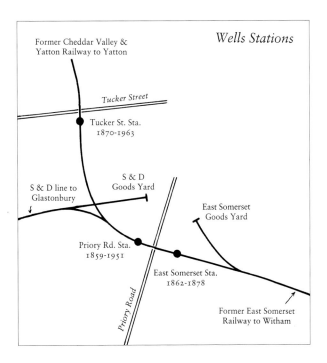

Wells East Somerset. The former station when in later use as a cheese store. Note the GWR horse drawn wagons.

WELLS EAST SOMERSET

OPENED: 1st March 1862 (as the terminus of the Shepton Mallet - Wells section of the East Somerset Railway).

CLOSED: Passengers - 1st January 1878 (with the commencement of through running on the former Cheddar Valley and East Somerset Railways over the short stretch of Somerset & Dorset Railway track).
Goods - 13th July 1964 (freight trains, mostly carrying stone continued to pass through until 29th April 1969).

Opened in 1862 as the terminus of the East Somerset Railway from Witham, this, the second station to open in Wells, was sited on the east side of Priory Road less than 100 yds from the terminus of the Somerset Central's line from Glastonbury to Wells opened three years earlier. It was described at the time as a 'light and neat structure, with a glass awning, erected by a local builder'. The first train carrying directors and officials, including representatives of the GWR, ran on the last day of February 1862 and was met at the terminus by a local band and the Mayor and Corporation of Wells. A celebration lunch was held at the Swan Hotel.

With the construction of the new spur line between the two stations across Priory Road and the commencement of through west-east services, the original East Somerset terminus closed to passengers in 1878. The former station building was, for some years, in use as a cheese store but was then destroyed by fire in 1929. The associated tracks became, for many years, the major goods yard for Wells: the East Somerset Yard.

Today virtually no trace of the railway can be seen east of Priory Road except for a small section of wall close to the former Railway Inn (now renamed the Sherston Inn). The trackbed of the former East Somerset line is taken over by a section of the Wells relief road appropriately named East Somerset Way.

WELLS PRIORY ROAD

OPENED: 15th March 1859 (with the opening of the Glastonbury - Wells section of the Somerset Central Railway).

CLOSED: Passengers - 29th October 1951 (with closure of the Glastonbury - Wells line).
Goods - 12th October 1964 (final years in use via a link to the GWR line from Yatton to Witham).
(Freight trains, mostly carrying stone, continued to pass through until 29th April 1969).

Opened as the terminus of the Glastonbury - Wells section of the Somerset Central Railway, the station was called Wells until October 1883 when the suffix 'Priory Road' was added. The opening of this link to Glastonbury was the result of pressure from the Wells traders for links to the Somerset Central line which had reached Glastonbury from Highbridge Wharf in 1854, thus providing a link to the Bristol area via the GWR, through interchange at the Highbridge Stations.

The formal opening of the line on 3rd March 1859 was accompanied by processions, triumphal arches

Wells Priory Road. A push-pull set under the timber train shed in about 1935. The main station facilities are in the building to the left

and feasting in the cathedral city.

Priory Road itself had only a single platform, but this was covered in part by a timber train shed. The buildings on the station site were constructed of both brick and stone, the station building being of local Mendip stone. A number of facilities were provided, including waiting rooms (one for ladies only), booking office and station master's office. The level of passenger traffic was never high but the station was regularly used by school children at Wells Cathedral School and the Blue School. By the early 1950s passenger traffic on the Glastonbury line had reduced to practically none and Priory Road Station closed in 1951. Soon afterwards the train shed roof was demolished.

A goods yard operated to the north of the station building. Following closure of the link to Glastonbury adjustments were made to bring links to the still open GWR through line between Yatton and Witham. However with the closure of the latter, trade ceased. The stone built goods shed was demolished in 1988, the materials being used at Cranmore on the restored East Somerset Railway

whilst the wooden shed attached to it was re-erected at Washford by the Somerset & Dorset Railway Trust.

Today virtually nothing remains on the Priory Road site. The trackbed north to Tucker Street has also been taken over by a section of the Wells relief road and given the appropriate name of Strawberry Way, a fitting reminder of the old 'Strawberry Line', as the Cheddar Valley Line was affectionately known. The station site is in use by Travers Perkins and a supermarket. Small remnants of station walls are all that remain.

WELLS TUCKER STREET

OPENED: 5th April 1870 (with the opening of the Cheddar - Wells section of the Cheddar Valley and Yatton Railway).

CLOSED: Passengers - 9th September 1963 (with closure of the Yatton -Witham line to passenger traffic). Goods - 13th July 1964 (freight trains, mostly carrying stone, continued to pass through until 29th April 1969).

This was the original southern limit of the Cheddar Valley broad gauge branch line from Yatton. It was named Wells until 12th July 1920 when the suffix

Wells Tucker Street. The principal 1870s building on the down (north) side of the track. Note the enamel advertisement boards and milk churns.

'Tucker Street' was added; it reverted to Wells from 6th May 1950 until closure in 1963.

The station was built of local stone at a time when flamboyant Victorian architecture was at its height, and this was reflected in the artistic attention given to ridge tiles, barge boards and even chimney pots. With its original broad gauge layout, the two platforms were widely spaced, with the main buildings on the north side of a curved section of track. Canopies and waiting rooms were provided on both platforms though the building on the up platform (towards Yatton) was of a later date.

Weston (Bath). The attractive building on the north side of the line; it survives today used by the radio station, Bath F.M.

Both passenger and goods traffic was relatively good and certainly better than at the Priory Road Station. The goods facilities, including a large goods shed, were north of the station beyond the Tucker Street road bridge. A number of assorted railway buildings were dotted around the station site including a row of railway cottages behind the station on the town side and adjacent to the wide approach road.

As noted above, in the account of Priory Road Station, the trackbed is now taken up by a section of the Wells relief road, Strawberry Way. The station buildings have now gone but the railway cottages, with characteristic railings, are still in residential use. The goods shed is the only significant building to survive. The nearby Cheddar Valley Inn, on Tucker Street, with a sign illustrating a train at Cheddar Station, is also a reminder of a past era.

WESTON (BATH)

OPENED: 4th August 1869 (with the opening of the Mangotsfield (Glos) - Bath branch from the Bristol - Gloucester line).
CLOSED: Passengers - 21st September 1953.
Goods - 29th November 1965.

Weston Station served the western outskirts of Bath; the old village of Weston being about a mile from the station to the west. It opened as Weston but was renamed Weston (Bath) on 1st October 1934. The main stone built building was on the down (north) line, it comprised two pavilion structures at right angles to the tracks with elaborate barge boards. In the recess between these sections was an iron canopy. The building was not entirely symmetrical as it had an annex at the west end. The shelter on the up platform was originally timber framed but in later years this was replaced by a red brick structure. The down platform was 600 ft in length - twice that of the up; this was particularly useful when long excursion trains for the S & D started from Weston. During the First World War hospital trains arrived at Weston (Bath), with injured servicemen being taken to the Bath War Hospital at Combe Park on the site of the present Royal United Hospital.

The opening of the Bath Electric Tramway in 1904 had a major impact on passenger numbers as the trams offered a more frequent and cheaper service into the city centre. Most rail passengers at this time travelled westwards towards Bristol. Records show that just prior to its closure in September 1953 only

Weston Milton. A view east in 1963 of the two concrete platforms with shelters before the Weston-super-Mare loop line was singled on this section in 1972.

about a dozen passengers used the station each day.

In about 1945 the staff consisted of a station master and porter. The station master lived in a house to the west of the station at the junction of Ashley Avenue and Station Road which had similar barge boards to the main station building. Weston had one siding to the south of the line opposite the station: its principal traffic was coal. A signal box was sited just west of the Station Road level crossing.

Today the main station building survives in use by Bath F.M. It remains in good condition, complete with barge boards, and has an extension at the west end. All trace of the trackbed has gone beneath major industrial developments immediately south of the station building. The former station house survives in residential use as no. 16 Station Road; alongside the house two posts, originally part of the level crossing, are still in place. West of the level crossing the former trackbed is in use as a walkway.

WESTON JUNCTION

OPENED: 14th June 1841 (at the junction of the spur line to Weston-super-Mare opening with the Bristol - Bridgwater section of the Bristol & Exeter Railway).
CLOSED: 1st March 1884 (with the closure of the spur line to Weston-super-Mare and its replacement by the new loop line).

This small station opened in 1841 at the junction of the Weston-super-Mare branch line with the Bristol to Bridgwater first section of the B & E Railway. A platform, ticket office and primitive waiting room were provided serving passengers transferring to and from branch line trains (initially horse drawn) and the main line services. The Junction Station did not have a good reputation - a local book published in 1855 stated 'There was often a lot of tiresome waiting at this place' whilst the 1877 *Visitors' Handbook* noted 'it must be regretted that the Junction shed often fails in affording adequate protection to the luggage of travellers'. There were plans to improve facilities at the same time as the second Weston-super-Mare Station opened in 1866 but these never came to fruition. The station closed on 1st March 1884 with the opening of the new loop line and the closure of the branch. No photograph exists of the station.

WESTON MILTON

OPENED: 3rd July 1933 (on the Weston-super-Mare loop line originally opened through this site in 1884).
CLOSED: Remains open for passenger services on the Bristol - Weston-super-Mare - Taunton line.

This small station opened on the Weston-super-Mare loop line to serve the growing suburbs of the resort. The suffix halt was dropped as from 5th May 1969. With singling of this section of the loop line in 1972, the redundant platform was moved to the new Lymstone Commando Station on the Exmouth branch in Devon.

In 1983 the station was refurbished at a cost of £30,000, a brick shelter being provided on the platform and also an enlarged car park for about forty cars. Today it is served by local trains on the Bristol - Weston-super-Mare - Taunton line and also, one up and one down through London Paddington trains in the morning and evening peaks, the platform being long enough to accommodate inter-city trains (unlike the nearby Worle Parkway).

WESTON-SUPER-MARE

FIRST STATION

OPENED: 14th June 1841 (as the terminus of the
  Weston-super-Mare spur line opened with the Bristol
  - Bridgwater section of the Bristol & Exeter
  Railway).

CLOSED: 20th July 1866 (with its replacement by the
  second, larger, station on the slightly shortened spur
  line).

SECOND STATION

OPENED: 20th July 1866 (as the replacement, larger,
  station on the spur line originally opened in 1841).

CLOSED: 1st March 1884 (with the closure of the spur
  line and its replacement by the Weston-super-Mare
  loop line).

THIRD STATION

OPENED: 1st March 1884 (with the opening of the
  Weston-super-Mare loop line).

CLOSED: Passengers - remains open for services on the
  Bristol - Taunton - Exeter line.
  Goods - 20th June 1966.

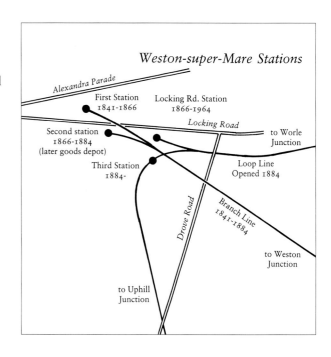

When the Parliamentary Act establishing the B & E Railway received its Royal Assent in 1836, no railway into Weston-super-Mare itself was envisaged. Local opinion was against having 'noisy, smoking, steam engines' in the then small, but growing resort. It was only following a second Act of Parliament in 1838 that the town gained its own branch line which opened on the same day, 14th June 1841, as the first section to Bridgwater of the main line from Bristol to Exeter. The coming of the railway was, without doubt, the most significant event in the town's early history. The concerns regarding steam engines were resolved by mainly using horses.

The branch line, leaving the main line at Weston Junction, followed the alignment of what is now

Weston-super-Mare (1st station). A pencil sketch of the first station by an unknown artist dated 23rd September 1846.

Winterstoke Road to a terminus station at the west end of Alexandra Parade, at the site of today's floral clock. The route to the single storey gothic type building designed by Brunel, included a level crossing over Locking Road. The station was a small but neat stone structure with a clock tower but there was no waiting room nor refreshment facilities on the single platform. Passengers travelled in small open-sided horse drawn carriages, each train comprising two or three four wheeled coaches drawn by three horses in tandem. It was said that this journey, against a head wind, could take up to half-an-hour and some preferred to walk. From 1848 a locomotive hauled train worked from Weston-super-Mare to Bristol in the mornings with a corresponding down train in the evenings. Other services were still worked by horses. During 1850 a steam engine and carriage operated during daylight, horses still being used at night, being quieter. On 1st April 1851 steam operation took over entirely.

With the growing passenger and goods traffic on this primitive line, extra facilities were needed at the station and in 1862 the first goods were despatched from a separate goods shed, some 140 ft long and 60 ft wide, on the south side of Locking Road. By the early 1860s it was obvious, with the accelerating growth of the town, that the small single track station was inadequate. A second station, designed by Francis Fox, the B & E's chief engineer, was built, this time on the south side of Locking Road, thus eliminating the level crossing

Weston-super-Mare (2nd station). A view of the main passenger entrance to the second station in about 1875.

which had been the scene of a number of accidents. The new station on a site now covered by the Tesco store behind the cinema, and accessed off Locking Road to the north, was still a terminus on the original branch line, but a second track had been laid. The much larger, lofty station building, built at a cost of £10,000 by Mr Brock of Bristol, had two platforms as well as sidings. The platform was 420 ft long, the building overall was 243 ft long and 100 ft wide. A visitor's handbook of 1877 stated, 'The station itself is thoroughly well arranged and managed with a general attention to the needs and reasonable wishes of visitors'. The first station on Alexandra Parade was demolished and the land sold in 1867. The area for some years was known as Station Square.

Still the facilities proved inadequate and plans were prepared for the construction of a new loop line into the resort and the abandonment of the original branch. It was considered urgent to place the resort on a main line rather than a branch. An Act of Parliament was passed in 1875 but the loop line did not open for another nine years. Built with standard gauge track, it opened on 1st March 1884. The architect for the third station, costing some £110,000 for the station site and approaches, was again Francis Fox, the contractor being Mr. J. Hartley of Birmingham. Extracts from the *Weston Mercury* of 1st March 1884 provide a good description of the stone building '. . . its appearance inside and out is decidedly pleasing and effective. It is a long low building Gothic in style . . . a very good effect being produced by the height of the towers

above the bridge staircases. The platforms are roofed in what is known as the 'veranda' pattern, the lines being left uncovered. The up platform is 270 yds in length and the roof is constructed of girders and cantilevers, supported by cast iron columns and covered in entirety by rough rolled plate glass. The whole of the cast iron work is painted to represent bronze and the effect produced is rather pretty. Adjoining the up platform there are first, second and third class waiting rooms, booking offices and an excellent refreshment room provided with kitchens and all the apparatus necessary to meet the wants of passengers. No expense has been spared in providing a suitable bridge and it is considered to be one of the best on the line. It is built of lattice girders, encased with match boarding, the whole being covered in so on to afford complete shelter from the weather . . . The platform on the down side is 230 yds in length,

Weston super-Mare (3rd station). Passengers on the up platform in about 1900. Note the intricate glazed canopies.

the roofing being similar to that on the up side. The only offices on the down side are a cloak room, ladies' waiting room and general waiting room. Both platforms are paved with Staffordshire vitrified chequered blue tiles . . . Considerable shelter from the wind is provided by the screens which have been erected at the end of the roofing. No expense has been spared in making all the offices as replete as possible; new furniture has been provided for the first class waiting room which is fitted up in an elegant style whilst the furniture from the old station has been newly upholstered and varnished for use in the other waiting rooms . . . The station is approached from the Walliscote Road by a road 40 ft wide and this widens out into a fine open space - in fact a finer station yard we have rarely seen . . . Passengers on alighting from their cabs will be protected from rain by the veranda roof. Short trains for Bristol will start from a dock line on the inner side of the up platform'. Remarkably, many of these features survive today.

For a time the old 1866 station was used for band concerts before being converted for use as a goods station. Alongside the Locking Road wall were stables which housed the horses which drew GWR carts on deliveries around the town. The goods station suffered severe bomb damage in June 1942 which destroyed the roof but it remained in use until 20th June 1966 when goods facilities were withdrawn from the town.

Known since its opening as Weston-super-Mare General, it lost its suffix from 21st September 1953 but regained it again from 6th May 1958, only to lose it again when Locking Road excursion station closed on 6th September 1964. In 1986 the station underwent a major face-lift and early in the 1990s extensive work was undertaken on the glazed canopy roofs. This followed a time when the future of this historic station building had seemed in doubt. Much of the canopy iron work and glazing was replaced by modern materials, but retaining the original basic ridge and furrow design. The main offices continue today on the up platform with a modernised booking office, a bar/café, 'Off the Rails', and a waiting room. The bay platform is no longer in use though the track remains, used for storage of rolling stock. No facilities are provided on the down platform. The station has good local services on the Bristol - Taunton - Exeter line and some inter-city services direct to London Paddington, the Midlands, the North and the West Country. The operation of the station is handicapped to some degree by the loop line, apart from through the station itself, being only single track, having been singled by 1972. Plans have been made to restore the double track but as yet this has not been implemented. In 1984 the 1862 goods shed and the remains of the 1866 station were both demolished with the development of the Tesco supermarket and Hildesheim Court. Much of the 1866 station had already been removed in 1977. Small sections of the 1866 station wall remain today on Station Road and Locking Road.

WESTON-SUPER-MARE ASHCOMBE ROAD

Weston, Clevedon & Portishead Light Railway (*see p 149*)

WESTON-SUPER-MARE LOCKING ROAD

OPENED: 1866 (As an additional facility for excursion traffic adjacent to the second Weston-super-Mare station. A major development of the platform into a full station facility opened in 1914).
CLOSED: 6th September 1964.

Excursion traffic has always been a feature of the railway scene at Weston-super-Mare. Even in 1844 it was estimated that 25,000 passengers travelled to the resort by train. By 1851 the B & E Railway introduced its own day trips, initially from Bristol, and on Whit Monday of that year 2000 excursionists arrived by train. In 1866 the second station included in its layout a separate excursion platform and outside the station was a hall where tea was provided for visitors at 1½d a cup; the return fare from Bristol at that time was 1/6d.

When the 1884 station was constructed, the 1866 excursion platform was retained and developed. This was now long enough to accommodate a whole excursion train and extended from the west end of Locking Road nearly to the Drove Road railway bridge. Re-building took place in 1907, the width of the platform being doubled and a bay line laid along the platform rear. Three shelters were also provided. On 8th April 1914 a new excursion station was opened, a major development of the old excursion platform with direct road access onto Locking Road. The name Weston-super-Mare Locking Road was formally used from 1930. The four platforms were used primarily during the summer months and the station had its own ticket office and waiting room. It served not only visitors to the seaside attractions but also, on occasions, trains bringing delegates to conferences at the resort. On some Bank Holidays it was reported that up to 30,000 visitors were brought

Weston-super-Mare Locking Road. Passengers disembarking from a train arrived at Platform 2 of the excursion station in about 1924.

to Weston-super-Mare in thirty special trains.

By the 1960s, however, most day trippers were coming to the resort by car or coach and Locking Road closed in 1964 and was demolished in 1967. Ironically, the site is now used for car and coach parking.

West Pennard. Looking east towards the A361 bridge. The station house (right) and goods shed (left) remain today in residential and storage use respectively.

WEST PENNARD

OPENED: 3rd February 1862 (with the opening of the Glastonbury - Cole section of the Somerset Central Railway).

CLOSED: Passengers - 7th March 1966 (with closure of the Evercreech Junction - Highbridge line to passenger traffic).

Goods - 10th June 1963.

Like many other stations on the Highbridge - Glastonbury - Cole Somerset Central Railway, West Pennard Station was sited some way from the village it primarily served; in this case nearly two miles north east along the A361. A long loop was installed at this point with the high roofed stone buildings with tall chimneys incorporating a waiting room, booking office and staff accommodation on the up (south) platform. Two smaller buildings were on this platform at the east end, one being a tariff (or goods) shed. Behind, and to the west of, the platform stood the station master's house. A large wooden waiting shelter, with fretted canopy, stood on the down platform; at the eastern end of this platform was a large stone goods shed with a through loop siding continuing behind the platform itself. The adjacent goods yard, served by a siding, included a cattle loading dock, cattle pens, coal bins and a seven ton hand crane. As at many rural stations, coal and milk traffic were particularly important. The wooden

Whitchurch Halt. Looking south from the A37 bridge at the 1925 halt with GWR pagoda hut.

signal box stood off the west end of the up platform; this closed on 26th August 1964, at which time the down loop line and all sidings were taken out of use. West Pennard ceased to be staffed on 25th June 1962 and was re-designated as a halt.

Following closure of the goods yard and the withdrawal of passenger services in 1966, the station buildings were eventually purchased in 1987, and are now the base for a transport company, R. C. Withers, with the owners living in the former station master's house. The station building has been converted into a house and the former goods shed, with a major extension, is used for storage.

WHITCHURCH HALT

OPENED: 1st January 1925 (on the Bristol - Radstock line originally opened through this site in 1873).
CLOSED: 2nd November 1959.

The halt was built on open ground in a shallow cutting south of the A37 stone built road bridge over the railway. It mainly served the village of Whitchurch to the north and access to the simple platform was from the west side of the road bridge. Illumination was provided by oil lamps on two unusual standards which incorporated a step on which the guards of stopping trains could stand while lighting, extinguishing or changing the lamps.

The station and platform have now vanished with the shallow cutting filled in. A gap in the stone parapet filled with a small section of wooden fence on the A37 bridge marks the former entrance to the halt's access footpath.

WICK ST. LAWRENCE

Weston, Clevedon & Portishead Light Railway (*see p 150*)

WILLITON

OPENED: 31st March 1862 (with the opening of the West Somerset Railway from Norton Junction to Watchet).
CLOSED: Passengers - 4th January 1971 (with closure of the Norton Fitzwarren - Minehead line).
Goods - 6th July 1964.
REOPENED: 28th August 1976 (with the reopening of the Blue Anchor - Williton section of the restored West Somerset Railway).

The station, nearly a mile east of the town itself, originally had one platform with a stone station building and goods shed on what is now the down side towards Minehead. The building incorporated a waiting room, booking hall and office and small station master's office. In 1874, twelve years after its opening, a passing loop and up platform were added, the latter with an all timber waiting room of typical B & E design, including decorative barge boards. The new platform was slightly longer than the original but this latter was also extended in 1874. The passing loop itself was extended towards Watchet in 1907 and 1937 but the platforms were not extended. A covered wooden footbridge was erected, linking to the down platform between the main building and the goods shed. This was replaced in the 1920s by a metal lattice type bridge located between the main building and the signal box. This box, dating from 1875, was sited at the southern end of the down platform adjacent to a small level crossing serving local traffic. The use of this level crossing had reduced after the construction of a road overbridge south of the station by the B & E Company in 1873. The main goods facilities were to the west of the station, one siding serving the goods shed and cattle pens and another longer siding serving a loading platform. Sugar beet and timber went out, fertiliser and coal came in. Other features of the station included a large brick built water tower with a cast iron tank close to the road bridge, an adjacent small stone 1862 building (half coal shed/half office) and a wooden parcels office on the down platform.

Since its reopening by the West Somerset Railway in 1976, the main station building has been extensively renovated. The booking office and waiting room have been restored to their original condition, including the furniture. The up side waiting room is now in good condition in use as a small shop for sales of books and refreshments. Pride of place goes to the signal box, which had closed in 1971, now restored to use, and the only former

Williton. An early view of the flooded line towards Watchet, with the first footbridge beyond the main station buildings (left) and shelter. Both of these buildings remain today on the West Somerset Railway.

B & E box in full working order. The large 1862 goods shed for some years was the principal focus of work by the Diesel and Electric Preservation Group. More recently this work has been transferred to a large new steel building on the former goods yard. The operational development of the new building has been supported by the Heritage Lottery Fund. It is planned to use the old goods shed as a museum/display area.

The other major feature of the current railway scene at Williton Station is the pre-fabricated steel framed vault roofed building at the north end of the former goods yard. Originally built in 1899 and now Grade II listed, it stood until 1992 in the GWR Swindon Works. Following protracted negotiations, it was then transferred to Williton in sections and re-erected. It is now rail connected and used for the storage and restoration of locomotives and other rolling stock. In 2001 new GWR style lighting was installed at the station.

Following demolition of the second bridge in the 1960s, access between the platforms has been via the level crossing at the southern end. Early in the 1990s,

the GWR footbridge at Trowbridge was purchased and brought to Williton. Some restoration has taken place and it is hoped that it will be re-erected shortly on the site of the original wooden bridge.

WINCANTON
OPENED: 3rd February 1862 (with the opening of the Cole - Templecombe section of the Dorset Central Railway).
CLOSED: Passengers - 7th March 1966 (with closure of the Bath Green Park - Poole line to passenger traffic).
Goods - 5th April 1965 (except sidings to local creamery which closed 3rd January 1966).

Located on the western side of the market town, Wincanton was somewhat unusual in layout, the platforms being staggered, overlapping for only 120 ft. The principal building, with a typical S & D angled canopy, and incorporating general and ladies' waiting rooms, booking office, store rooms and a station master's house, was sited at the southern end of the 240 ft down platform. A footbridge from the middle of this platform linked to the extreme northern end of the long (450 ft) up platform, on which only a small shelter with a canopy, was provided. A signal box stood adjacent to, and

Wincanton. Looking north towards Evercreech Junction on 29th July 1962. Unusually the platforms are staggered with an overlap of only 120 ft.

behind, this shelter. The original footbridge was of open lattice design, but in later years this was replaced by a standard Southern Railway concrete open bridge. Wincanton was one of the first stations in Somerset to be illuminated by gas, though later this was replaced by electric lamps mounted on Southern Railway concrete posts.

A goods yard, south of the station on the down side, beyond the main station buildings included a large goods shed. The yard, for many years, handled a large volume of horse box traffic associated with Wincanton Race Course. A cattle dock and pens served the local agricultural community. In 1933 the Cow and Gate sidings opened, serving the adjacent new milk depot and creamery. Considerable milk traffic was handled with movements to the London area via Templecombe and Salisbury. The

depot/creamery survived until the late 1980s, latterly as a Unigate factory, making various dairy products.

Goods traffic generally ceased at Wincanton as from April 1965 though the creamery sidings remained in use until 3rd January 1966.

Today all traces of the station and adjoining goods yard have gone. Some remnants could be seen until the mid 1980s but housing now covers the whole area. Leading off Station Road is the aptly named Pines Close and the foundations of the old signal box remain in the garden of one of the houses.

WINSCOMBE

OPENED: 3rd August 1869 (with the opening of the Yatton - Cheddar section of the Cheddar Valley & Yatton Railway).

CLOSED: Passengers - 9th September 1963 (with closure of the Yatton - Witham line to passenger traffic). Goods - 10th June 1963.

Unlike other stations on the Cheddar Valley line, Winscombe was not provided with a substantial building at its opening. The original station, known as Woodborough for the first four months until 1st December 1869, was a simple wooden structure sited west of Winscombe, north of the railway bridge over the A371 to Weston-super-Mare. This small

Winscombe. Second station, looking south. The platform now forms part of the Old Station Millennium Green.

building was replaced by a new building of a then typical GWR style opened on 9th January 1905. Like the earlier building, the platform and brick building with a glazed canopy was sited on the east side of the line at the end of an approach road up from the A371. This building included a booking office and waiting room, a ladies' waiting room, a parcels office and a gentlemen's toilet. A large corrugated shed provided further storage space at the north end of the platform.

A short dock siding ran behind the platform at the Yatton (north) end. Also to the north of the station was a loop and a further short siding. As with many stations on the line, a camping coach was often sited in the dock siding. The suffix 'Somerset' had been added on 12th January 1906.

Overall the level of passenger traffic was slightly higher at Winscombe than at other stations on the line; in 1903 18,870 passenger tickets were issued; by 1933 the figure had fallen to 5,234.

Following closure of the station to both passengers and goods in 1963, the station building was demolished; however the platform and sections of railings/gates remained on the Cheddar Valley Railway Walkway that was developed over the line's formation from Yatton through Congresbury to Axbridge and Cheddar.

In 2000 the station site was renovated by Winscombe and Sandford Parish Council as the Old Station Millennium Green. The Green now includes the renovated station platform on which are GWR seats and sections of the former station gates and railings. The foundations of the former station building have also been exposed. All this forms a striking feature on the well used Railway Walkway.

Witham. The 1875 rebuilt station looking towards Frome in about 1908. The main station offices and station master's house are through the bridge on the up platform.

WITHAM

OPENED: 1st September 1856 (with the opening of the Frome - Yeovil section of the Wilts, Somerset & Weymouth Railway).

CLOSED: Passengers - 3rd October 1966.
    Goods - 30th December 1963.

Witham Station, some five miles south west of Frome, originally opened on the single track broad gauge line from Westbury to Yeovil. One platform and a passing loop were provided. Two years later, in 1858, the first section of the East Somerset Railway to Shepton Mallet opened and Witham took on a new role as a junction station.

Following gauge conversion of the original single track in June 1874, the Frome to Witham line was doubled in 1875; the Witham to Castle Cary section followed in 1880. With the doubling of the tracks Witham Station was rebuilt, the original platform (now down) being incorporated.

Following the rebuilding, the station layout included two platforms. There was a platform canopy on the up side and a wooden building housed the principal offices. A slate hung station master's house also stood on the up platform and further structures included an iron lamp room and cast iron gent's urinal.

Branch services along the East Somerset Railway used a bay platform behind the up platform leading in from the south. This bay was unusual in having a short length covered by an overall wooden shed with a canopy on the side providing cover for a section of

Wiveliscombe. A view south west including the main building, on the up platform. This survives today, complete with bay window, in use as an office on an industrial development.

the main up platform. The wooden shed covering little more than one carriage length, in the middle of a train, was built in 1869.

A stone built waiting room with a tall Brunel type chimney, together with a small wooden shed built in 1888 for passenger train parcels, stood on the original down platform. An 1887 iron open footbridge crossed the main lines connecting the centres of the two platforms. Passenger numbers were never very high ranging from 13,015 tickets issued in 1903 to 5,703 in 1933. In the 1920s and 1930s about twelve men were employed; back in 1863 there were only five.

Goods sidings were extensive in the area, mainly linked with stone traffic from the Shepton Mallet line. At the station itself there was a small fan of five sidings for local traffic behind the down platform plus sidings on the up side. The goods facilities were withdrawn in October 1966.

The suffix 'Somerset' was belatedly added to the station nameboards as from 9th June 1958 to distinguish it from another station of the same name in Essex. Eight years later the station closed to passengers and was soon demolished. The wooden branch line train shed had been taken down earlier in about 1960. Passenger services were withdrawn from the line to Shepton Mallet and Wells as from 9th September 1963. The former station site can be seen but no significant remnants of the station can be traced. The adjacent railway cottages remain in residential use, one with the name 'Station House'.

WIVELISCOMBE

OPENED: 8th June 1871 (with the opening of the Norton Junction - Wiveliscombe section of the Devon and Somerset Railway).
CLOSED: Passengers - 3rd October 1966 (with closure of the Norton Fitzwarren - Barnstaple line). Goods - 6th July 1964.

Sited to the east of the town, where the Barnstaple line swings sharply south, Wiveliscombe was the terminus of the branch for just over two years from June 1871 until November 1873 when the continuation to Barnstaple was opened.

As the temporary terminus, Wiveliscombe was provided with a turntable which was later transferred to Barnstaple. It was one of the original passing stations when the line was completed. The local stone station buildings, of similar design to those at Milverton, were on the up platform and included booking offices with an attractive bay window on the platform side. On the down side there was only a waiting shelter. In 1903 20,613 passenger tickets were issued; this fell to 11,886 by 1933. A brick built goods shed was served by a siding leading from the up line at the Taunton end. Beyond this was a large timber signal box behind which were sidings and a goods yard. An earlier signal box at the Barnstaple end of the up platform became redundant in 1906. The crossing loops through the station were extended three times during the station's life in 1906, 1911, and 1939.

Station Road now leads into industrial development. The former main station building, complete with bay window, is in use as an office. A small section of platform survives as does the goods shed with canopy, now in industrial use.

WOOKEY

OPENED: 1st August 1871 (on the Cheddar - Wells section of the Cheddar Valley & Yatton Railway originally opened through this site on 5th April 1870).
CLOSED: Passengers - 9th September 1963 (with closure of the Yatton - Witham line to passenger traffic). Goods - 10th June 1963 (except for private siding traffic to nearby paper mills).

Wookey Station was sited to the north of the village alongside the road leading to Wookey Hole caves and paper works, both of which generated significant traffic. A dedicated track ran to the paper mills from 1879 to 1965. The platform and small building were on the south side of the single track line. The building with waiting room and booking office was smaller than many on the line and was dominated by a large goods shed, its size indicative of great expectations of goods traffic! The small signal box at the east end of the platform was set forward to give signalmen a better view through the adjoining road over bridge. Passenger ticket sales were always relatively low: 8,322 in 1903 down to 1,789 in 1933.

Today the goods shed remains within an industrial development, Station Yard, but the station building and signal box have gone. The old station house survives south of the line on the east side of the Wookey Hole road.

Wookey. Looking towards Wells in about 1960.

WORLE

OPENED: 1st March 1884 (with the opening of the Weston-super-Mare loop line).

CLOSED: 2nd January 1922.

Worle opened with the Weston-super-Mare loop line in March 1884. The station, with the main building on the up side, was built by H. W. Pollard of Bridgwater. It was much nearer to the village of Worle than the main line station at St George's (see account of Puxton and Worle) which had previously served the village. It closed in 1922 though the disused main building and platform remained in place for some forty years until demolition in the mid 1960s. No close up photograph of the station is known to exist.

Worle. The disused station in 1934, twelve years after its closure.

Worle Parkway. The inaugural train, on which the author was a passenger, at the down platform on 24th September 1990.

WORLE PARKWAY

OPENED: 24th September 1990 (on the Bristol - Taunton - Exeter line originally opened through this site in 1841)

CLOSED: Remains open for passenger services on the Bristol - Weston-super-Mare - Taunton line.

Built at a cost of £700,000, this modern station was developed as a joint initiative between British Rail and Avon County Council. Lightweight construction materials were used as far as possible due to its siting on marshy ground. A ramped footbridge, suitable for disabled passengers, links the two platforms on which metal and glass shelters are provided. On the north side is a large car park with spaces for two hundred cars. Designed mainly for use by residents in the North Worle and Locking Castle housing

areas, the station is served by local trains on the Bristol - Weston-super-Mare - Taunton line. No inter-city services stop, the platforms not being long enough to accommodate the full length of the trains.

Wrington. Looking east at the small red brick station similar in design to Langford and Blagdon, also on the Wrington Vale Light Railway.

WORLE TOWN
Weston, Clevedon & Portishead Light Railway (*see p 150*)

WRINGTON
OPENED: 4th December 1901 (with the opening of the Wrington Vale Light Railway from Congresbury to Blagdon).

CLOSED: Passengers - 14th September 1931 (with closure of the Wrington Vale Light Railway to passenger traffic).

Goods - 10th June 1963 (with closure of the Congresbury - Wrington section of the Wrington Vale Light Railway to goods traffic).

Wrington Station, the first on the Wrington Vale Light Railway after it left the Cheddar Valley line at Congresbury, was sited in the south of the village off Station Road. The building, similar to those at Blagdon and Langford also on the Wrington Vale line, was constructed of red brick and timber with a zinc roof surmounted by two chimneys. The roof continued downwards forming a small canopy. The platform, on the north side of the track, was some 150 ft long but only 2 ft 6 inches high. A corrugated iron parcels shed and oil lamps completed the facilities. Just beyond the station to the east was a loop line and goods siding on the down (north) side. A hand operated crane was available in the yard, the only station on the Wrington Vale Light Railway with a crane.

For some thirty years, from 1901 to 1931, the station provided services for passengers, particularly those travelling to Bristol via Congresbury and Yatton. However growing competition from the more direct bus service via the A38 led to a major decline in passengers; even by 1923 the number of passenger tickets issued had fallen to 6,061 from 11,020 in 1903. It is recorded that in 1926 on Mondays only a train left Wrington at 7.38 for the benefit of workers needing to reach Bristol before business hours. The Wrington Vale Light Railway remained open for goods (mainly coal) traffic as far as Wrington for some thirteen years after the rest of the line closed completely in 1950. After 1952 the line ended in buffer stops a short distance to the east of Wrington goods yard.

Today the station site is occupied by a veterinary centre and housing; one of the roads is called Old Station Close. The first house on the Close is called appropriately 'The Sidings'. Opposite the old station site a house is named 'The Signal Box', though no such facility ever existed at Wrington.

YATTON
OPENED: 14th June 1841 (with the opening of the Bristol - Bridgwater section of the Bristol & Exeter Railway).

CLOSED: Passengers - remains open for services on the Bristol - Weston-super-Mare - Taunton line.

Goods - 29th November 1965 (except for private sidings).

Opened as Clevedon Road on the first section of the B & E Railway in 1841, the name changed to Yatton on 28th July 1847 with the opening of the branch line to Clevedon. Substantial stone buildings of two different Brunel designs were erected on the up and down platforms; these survive today and are two of the best examples still in existence. It is possible that Brunel himself designed these two structures.

To accommodate Clevedon branch passenger trains, a bay was constructed at the west end of the up platform, its terminal end being covered by a large roof with louvres. This structure also provided cover for the west end of the up platform. In 1956 it was replaced by a more conventional canopy transferred from the bay platform at Dauntsey Station in Wiltshire. With the opening of the Cheddar Valley line to Winscombe, Axbridge and Cheddar in 1869, another bay was built at the west end; this time beside the down platform. A similar canopy was later constructed to shelter passengers using the west end of the main down platform and the Cheddar Valley bay. A short canopy was also added adjoining the east end of the down platform building. For a period in the 1910s and 1920s a GWR pagoda hut stood at the Bristol end of the up platform. An impressive covered footbridge linked the up and down platforms also at the Bristol end.

In its heyday Yatton was a busy station as it also acted as a major exchange station for passengers using the Clevedon and Cheddar Valley branches, the trains from which virtually all terminated in the bay platforms at Yatton. As from 1901 it also acted as an exchange point for passengers on the Wrington Valley line to Blagdon. Congresbury was the actual track junction from this branch with the Cheddar Valley line but most trains continued to Yatton. This important passenger role is confirmed by the number of tickets issued: 1903 55,958; 1913 57,177; 1923 59,898 and 1933 62,245. A later figure for 1956 recorded 96,000 passengers 'booked' and 136,000 outwards parcels, including mushroom traffic.

Yatton Station was also important for its goods facilities, with a large goods yard and shed south of the station behind the down and Cheddar Valley platforms. Apart from coal there was agricultural traffic such as implements, fertilisers, feeding stuffs and milk. Strawberries from the Cheddar Valley line and mushrooms from Wrington Vale also generated much goods traffic at Yatton. An engine shed opened in 1879 was accessed by a siding off the Clevedon branch north west of the station. It closed on 7th August 1960.

The scale of both passenger and goods activity is also indicated by the staff levels. In October 1920 the

Yatton. A Wells train in the Cheddar Valley bay platform on 15th April 1963. The later ex-Dauntsey canopy covers the west end of the up platform (left).

station master was supported by no less than forty staff including porters, clerks, ticket collectors and signalmen! This level of staffing continued until the 1950s. The station had the main facilities including the booking office and station master's office on the up platform and also, from 1888, a bookstall, (which survived until about the time of the closure of the Clevedon branch in 1966). In the 1920s the GWR employed a refreshment boy at Yatton to sell chocolates and cigarettes - he apparently wore a cap with word 'buffet'. A further feature was the large garden at the Bristol end of the down platform. A special display was mounted in 1953 for the Coronation.

Decline came in the late 1950s and 1960s, in particular with the closure of the Cheddar Valley and Clevedon lines, in 1963 and 1966 respectively. The Wrington Vale line had closed to passengers over thirty years earlier in 1931. The bay platforms were subsequently closed and the land re-used for car parking. The canopy over the down platform was removed as were the two water towers that for some years had dominated the down platform.

Yatton continues to serve a good number of passengers on the Bristol - Weston-super-Mare - Taunton line, including some direct inter-city trains to and from London Paddington. The two original 1841 buildings remain as does the ex Dauntsey canopy on the up platform. A VR post box is still in use on that platform. The roof has gone from the footbridge but the station garden has recently been renovated by local volunteers supported by three local firms. The former goods yard, closed in 1965, is now taken over by other commercial uses with two former railway buildings incorporated but not the goods shed (which has now gone). The Railway Inn continues to serve local residents and travellers and Station House, also on the up side, stands by the road bridge.

YEOVIL

Over the years five stations and halts have served this south Somerset town. Before these are examined in more detail, the following is a brief résumé of Yeovil's railway history.

The first railway to reach Yeovil was the B & E Railway's broad gauge branch line from Taunton and Durston which terminated at Yeovil Hendford Station on the western outskirts of the town in October 1853. The next arrival was the Wilts, Somerset & Weymouth Railway's broad gauge line from Westbury, Frome and Castle Cary terminating at Yeovil Pen Mill Station, in the east of the town, in September 1856; this line was completed to Weymouth soon after, opening in January 1857. Almost immediately afterwards, the B & E Railway extended its line across the south of the town to Pen Mill Station, opening on 2nd February 1857.

The third Company to serve Yeovil was the London & South Western Railway which had obtained powers principally to operate a line from Salisbury to Exeter running south of Yeovil but also a branch into the town itself. In the event, the line to Yeovil and the branch was completed first by the Salisbury & Yeovil Railway (operated by the L.S.W.R.) and ran northwards into the town, terminating at Yeovil Hendford Station, as from 1st June 1860. For the last three quarters of a mile the standard gauge track ran parallel to the B & E Railway's broad gauge link to Yeovil Pen Mill. Hendford Station only continued in this role for a short time until the new jointly financed (GWR and London & South Western Railway) Yeovil Town Station opened on 1st June 1861 at a point adjacent to the town centre where the London & South Western Railway and B & E lines converged. Until gauge conversion took place in the town in the mid 1870s, complicated mixed gauge working took place at Yeovil Town. From June 1861 Hendford Station was changed into a goods only station, though much later in 1932 Hendford Halt was opened to serve nearby industry and local residents.

Back on the London & South Western Railway the tracks to Exeter were completed and a new station, Yeovil Junction, opened in July 1860, with a new south west/north east spur leading into Yeovil. The original south east/north west curve from the Salisbury side was retained for several years but later abandoned. Although not for passenger use, a further station, Clifton Maybank Goods, was developed to the east of Yeovil Junction Station; it was used by both GWR and London & South Western Railway goods traffic and much exchange between the two companies took place here, linked also to the goods yard at Hendford.

Yeovil Stations

to Westbury & Paddington

Pen Mill 1856-

Hendford Halt 1932-1964

Hendford 1853-1861

Town 1861-1966

GWR

SR (LSWR)

to Taunton

Junction 1860-

to Waterloo

Clifton Maybank Goods

to Exeter

to Weymouth & Dorchester

YEOVIL HENDFORD

OPENED: 1st October 1853 (as the terminus of the Durston - Yeovil Hendford branch from the Bristol & Exeter Railway).

CLOSED: Passengers - 1st June 1861 (with the opening of Yeovil Town Joint Station which replaced the Hendford Station).

Goods - 9th October 1967.

YEOVIL HENDFORD HALT

OPENED: 2nd May 1932 (on the Durston - Yeovil branch originally opened through this site in 1853).

CLOSED: 15th June 1964 (with closure of the Taunton - Yeovil line to passenger traffic).

Yeovil Hendford Station opened in October 1853 as the terminus of the B & E's branch from Taunton. It

Yeovil Hendford Halt. Serving both local workers and residents, the concrete platform with small shelter opened in 1932.

Yeovil Hendford. The old station building which, following its closure in 1861, had various uses within the goods depot.

was located on the north side of the broad gauge line west of the A30 road bridge at the bottom of Hendford Hill. Built of stone with a timber roof, it also, for a short while from 1st June 1860, was the terminus of the Salisbury & Yeovil Railway line from Salisbury (operated by the L.S.W.R.) Following the opening of Yeovil Town Station in June 1861, Hendford Station became a goods depot with the old passenger building subsequently serving various goods storage uses. The depot closed on 9th October

1967. Over the years the whole area became more industrial, particularly associated with the Westland works. Hendford Halt, a concrete platform with a small shelter, again north of the line but a little to the west of the old station, opened in May 1932 to serve both local workers and residents using services on the Yeovil to Taunton branch line. It closed when passenger services ceased on the line in June 1964. The signal box opposite the halt closed just over a year later on 12th September 1965.

Today the whole area has been transformed by industrial uses and a new road. The site of the halt has gone but a footpath follows the route of the old railway towards Yeovil Town Station. The Railway Hotel, at the bottom of Hendford Hill, serves as a reminder of former rail activity in this part of Yeovil.

YEOVIL JUNCTION

OPENED: 19th July 1860 (with the opening of the Yeovil Junction - Exeter section of the London & South Western Railway).

CLOSED: Passengers - remains open for services on the London Waterloo - Salisbury - Exeter line. Goods - 5th April 1965

From its opening in July 1860, until a major rebuild in 1907-1909, Yeovil Junction comprised two island platforms between which ran a single through line. Two loop lines ran along the outer faces of the platforms; these lines served the main through passenger services, whilst the centre line was principally used by the branch line trains to and from

Yeovil Junction. The 1909 up side island platform containing the main station facilities looking west towards Sutton Bingham and Crewkerne.

Yeovil Town. Because of the curved track layout on the loops, 20 mph speed restrictions were imposed on the non-stop through trains.

As from 1909, a completely revised track and platform layout came into use at a cost of £50,000, with four through lines between two long island platforms, the outer platform faces being served by a loop line on the down side and by a long siding on the up side, with no direct connection to the up through line. The through trains on the London - Exeter line used the inner platform faces or, when non-stop, the two central lines. The outer platform faces were used by the branch line trains to Yeovil Town and by stopping trains to Salisbury. A covered lattice footbridge linked the platforms to the main approach road on the up side at the west end. A second footbridge spanning the tracks at the eastern end of the station was removed in 1920 and re-erected at Overton in Hampshire. The main station offices were, and still are, on the up platform (600 ft long). They were in two blocks - the western included stores, porters' room, station master's office, booking hall, general waiting room and bookstall. The eastern block contained a refreshment room, ladies' room and gentlemen's toilets. The down platform (520 ft long) buildings included a store room, guards' room, inspectors' office, general waiting room and gentlemen's toilets. All of these new buildings were constructed in red brick with red-glazed tile abutments. Between the Wars passenger traffic was at its maximum - in 1928 20,376 tickets were issued and 24,334 collected; by 1936 these figures had fallen to 15,358 and 21,105 respectively.

Goods facilities were laid out at Yeovil Junction for use both by the GWR on the south side and the London & South Western Railway (and Southern Railway) on the north. Goods sheds were in place in both yards; the south yard was linked to the Clifton Maybank goods station to the east of Yeovil Junction. Goods facilities were withdrawn generally as from 5th April 1965.

A large steam turntable was also sited near the goods shed on the south side. The west signal box remained in use until 30th April 1967; the east box is still there. Major changes at Yeovil Junction took place in the mid 1960s. The branch line passenger service to Yeovil Town ceased as from 2nd October 1966 and the replacement link to Yeovil Pen Mill only lasted until 4th May 1968. Much more significant was the unfortunate singling of much of the line from Yeovil to Exeter in April 1967. The down platform was closed and, because of the lack of a loop line on the north side, stopping trains could not pass at the station, only one platform face on the old up platform being useable. With track modification, this was rectified as from 26th March 1975 and both faces of the old up platform came into use for through trains. With the closure of the old down platform, the covered footbridge was truncated.

Today, much of the 1907-1909 rebuilding can be

Yeovil Pen Mill. Looking north showing the early overall timber roof. A down train stands at the platform, probably en route to Weymouth.

seen. The former up platform is in use for through trains between the West Country and London; the platform houses the booking office and the old refreshment room that displays many of the original features, including the windows and old counter. The down platform building remains in use. The goods sheds on both the down and up side are still in commercial use and the steam turntable is still there. Yeovil Junction is now the venue for special steam days and is the base for the Yeovil Steam Centre.

YEOVIL PEN MILL

OPENED: 1st September 1856 (with the opening of the Frome - Yeovil section of the Wilts, Somerset & Weymouth Railway).

CLOSED: Passengers - remains open for services on the Bristol - Westbury - Weymouth line
Goods - 12th September 1965

Opening in September 1856, Yeovil Pen Mill acted as a temporary terminus of the Wilts, Somerset & Weymouth Railway until the last stage of the line was opened to Weymouth in January 1857. B & E trains from Taunton and Durston also used the station from February 1857, running on a new link line across the town from Yeovil Hendford Station.

The principal buildings, constructed of the local Ham stone, sited on the up (north west) side, included the usual booking and other offices. The layout of the platforms is unusual with a single face up side platform and an island platform. Only the up line passes between the two platforms and the down line is served by the outer face of the island platform. The single line between the two platforms today serves the up trains to Castle Cary but also, in the past, was used by Taunton branch line trains – at that time it was signalled for use in both directions. Through running on this line has always been subject to severe speed restrictions because of a kink in the up platform. At one time a small bay platform was sited at the Castle Cary end on the up side; it was used for carriage storage and not by passenger trains.

From its early days, Pen Mill Station had an overall timber roof of a design similar to that at Frome, but this was replaced in 1934 by individual platform canopies. The platforms were also lengthened. The footbridge, originally under the roof, linking the up and island platforms was kept. A house was purchased for the station master in 1931 for £580.

Two signal boxes were erected in 1873, one north east of the station alongside the up line and a second to the south west in the fork between the Weymouth and Taunton lines. Both were closed in 1937, being then replaced by a large box at the Castle Cary end of the island platform.

For many years, and through to the 1950s, Yeovil Pen Mill was a hive of passenger activity. Through trains from London Paddington to Weymouth – including the Channel Islands Boat Expresses – stopped there, whilst local services ran to Chippenham and on the Bristol to Weymouth and

Yeovil Pen Mill. A view north on 3rd August 1959, showing the individual platform canopies which replaced the overall timber roof in 1934. Over forty years on, the station buildings are still almost identical to this picture.

Yeovil to Taunton lines. Summer services were particularly busy with passengers travelling to the Dorset coast and the refreshment rooms and station book stall were well patronised. In its heyday, Yeovil Pen Mill had a station master, a foreman, booking clerks and thirty-three other staff of various ranks.

Yeovil Pen Mill was also busy with goods traffic and a goods yard alongside the station on the down side handled large volumes of freight traffic. These included movements both to and from the Hendford goods depot and the Southern Railway goods facilities at Yeovil Junction. Sidings were also located alongside the up line to the north of the station; these served a large goods shed originally built in the broad gauge era. A siding linked to cattle pens south west of the station beyond the A30 road bridge; this was also the location for an engine shed which closed on 5th January 1959.

This shed closure marked the onset of a rapid decline in activity at Pen Mill. The boat trains ceased as from 2nd November 1959 with the trains to Weymouth being transferred to the London Waterloo to Dorset line; all through trains from Paddington ceased in 1960. The branch line trains to Taunton ceased with the closure of the branch line to passengers from 15th June 1964; local movements to Yeovil Town were withdrawn as from 29th November 1965. When this latter station closed, in October 1966, a new local connection from Pen Mill to Yeovil Junction commenced but this lasted less than two years until 4th May 1968. Finally, a significant factor affecting the remaining

passenger services on the Bristol to Weymouth line, was the singling of the Castle Cary to Yeovil and Yeovil to Maiden Newton tracks in May 1968. Yeovil Pen Mill had resumed a role it last played in the late 1850s as a passing point on the Westbury, Castle Cary and Weymouth line. Most of the extensive goods lines were also lifted during this period, the goods yard closing finally as from 12th September 1965. The signal box remains in use now and still today operates semaphore signals in the area around the station, some of the last remaining in the West Country.

Throughout this decline, the station buildings were largely unaltered; the covered footbridge and platform canopies remain though the small awning over the station entrance has gone. The booking office area was revamped and opened by the then local M. P., Paddy Ashdown, on 3rd December 1993. An independently run buffet operates in the original parcels office on the up platform. Nearby is the public house, The Great Western. Railway historians today consider that Yeovil Pen Mill, perhaps more than any other town station, retains the atmosphere of the old GWR days.

YEOVIL TOWN

OPENED: 1st June 1861 (on the Sherborne - Yeovil Hendford section of the Salisbury & Yeovil Railway originally opened through this site in 1860).
CLOSED: Passengers - 2nd October 1966 (with the final withdrawal of the shuttle service from Yeovil Junction).
Goods - 3rd May 1965.

This impressive station, adjacent to the town centre, opened in June 1861. Constructed as a joint venture

Yeovil Town. A view early in the 1900s of the imposing frontage; the roof line of the largest of the two original glazed train sheds can be seen above the building ridge line.

between the GWR and London & South Western Railway, it was on the line between Taunton and Yeovil Pen Mill and at the northern end of the branch line from the Salisbury to Exeter line. For many years it operated as a joint station with the two companies taking responsibility for different functions, for instance operation of the station and signalling (sounds familiar in 2002!). Indeed, at one time, there were two booking offices and two station masters, each having their own accommodation at either end of the station.

The fine symmetrical local stone structure, with the principal building containing the station offices and refreshment room on the north side, was rightly described at its opening as an impressive addition to the town's architecture. For much of its existence the station platforms - one for the GWR and two for the London & South Western Railway - were covered by two large glazed train sheds. One of these sheds covered all three platforms, whilst the other covered the remainder of the GWR platform which was longer (400 ft) then the London & South Western platforms (270 ft). Cast iron pillars held the roof aloft whilst bracing wires gave extra strength. As with all these train sheds, the glazing gave increasing problems through the years and the sheds were taken

Yeovil Town. A view in the early 1930s of the amazing tall glazed train shed that covered all three platforms.

Yeovil Town. A shuttle train to Yeovil Pen Mill in the late 1950s. Southern Railway canopies have replaced the lofty train shed.

down in the early 1930s, being replaced by individual steel platform canopies of Southern Railway style. The covered footbridge connecting the platforms remained.

Extensive goods facilities were provided both to the north west and south of the station. That to the north west was principally under the control of the London & South Western Railway and included a large goods shed and cattle pens. Three sidings immediately adjacent to the station were operated by the GWR. The main engine shed was to the south - a lofty building constructed of brick.

The signal box history was complex on account of the mixed GWR/London & South Western operations, originally on broad and standard gauge tracks. Four original boxes, a GWR and London & South Western box at either end of the station, were replaced by two boxes on 26th October 1902, one beside the Taunton branch and the other in the fork east of the station between the Yeovil Pen Mill and Yeovil Junction lines.

These two were again replaced by one box on 15th October 1916 at the Taunton end of the northern most GWR platform. This closed on 1st March 1967.

This box closure was the last main event in the decline and closure of the Town Station. This followed the successive withdrawal of passenger services to Taunton on 15th June 1964, to Yeovil Pen Mill on 29th November 1965 and to Yeovil Junction on 2nd October 1966. Local goods traffic also ceased in May 1965. Ironically some of the passenger traffic through the station had been lost to the rival Royal Blue Coach Services, which, in the 1950s and 1960s picked up passengers from stops outside the station. The station refreshment room benefited from the coach passengers but the trains did not!

Today the whole site has gone and there is no trace remaining of this impressive building. In 1970/71, soon after its acquisition, the Town Council decided on complete demolition and the site was used as a large car park for some thirty years. When visited in early 2002, the whole site was well advanced in redevelopment as a major new leisure park incorporating a multiplex cinema, health club etc. The only reminder of railway days is the continued presence of Newton Road bridge to the east of the station - its arches will now give access to a new car park. The former track bed to Pen Mill is in use as a railway walk.

WESTON, CLEVEDON & PORTISHEAD
LIGHT RAILWAY

The Weston, Clevedon & Portishead railway was promoted by local businessmen in order to address the problem of difficult rail travel between the three north Somerset resorts. When the scheme was originally conceived in the 1870s they were only served by branch lines from the Bristol & Exeter Railway, though in 1884 the Weston-super-Mare new loop line opened replacing the branch. Originally opened as a tramway, an Act of Parliament of 1899 authorised the line's conversion into a 'Light Railway'.

Passenger services commenced between Weston-super-Mare and Clevedon on 1st December 1897 with a scheduled journey time of 45 minutes. It was initially intended that the line would continue westwards as a tramway from the Weston-super-Mare terminus to the old Pier via the Boulevard; this was never completed and those sections laid were later removed. At the opening of the first section work had not commenced on the extension from Clevedon to Portishead, largely because of resistance from residents in the attractive Gordano Valley. This new section was eventually opened to passengers on 7th August 1907, a key role was serving quarries adjoining the Gordano Valley.

This new northern section proved to be a considerable financial burden; in 1910 the Company was placed in receivership. Competition from road transport increased and by the 1920s there were only four daily trains each way taking one hour from Weston-super-Mare to Portishead. The end came at 6.15 p.m. on 18th May 1940 when the last passenger train left Weston-super-Mare for Clevedon.

The principal stations on the Railway were at Weston-super-Mare, Clevedon and Portishead. Along the line was a series of small stations and halts; indeed there was a stopping point at virtually every site where the line crossed a road. Many of the intermediate stations and halts were no more than a small hut with or without a platform, access to trains in some cases being straight from ground level. Many of the huts and shelters on the line were made by Jennings of Bristol, manufacturers of portable buildings. From south to north the stations and halts were:

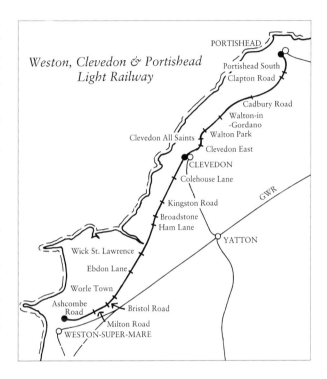

Weston, Clevedon & Portishead Light Railway

WESTON-SUPER-MARE – CLEVEDON
(Opened 1st December 1897 except where indicated)

WESTON-SUPER-MARE ASHCOMBE ROAD   Three quarters of a mile from the sea front; in early days a horse drawn carriage link to the old Pier; wooden station building (incorporating ticket office, waiting room and toilets) with unusual semi-circular corrugated iron roof; the original separate single short wooden platform (with shelter) only ten inches high but elevated platform erected in 1919; a cistern on four posts acted as a water-tower; limited sidings provided for goods wagons and spare coaches; former traffic manager's house now used as a chemist's shop.

MILTON ROAD HALT Asbestos covered shelter provided but no platform; siding of approx 130 yards.

BRISTOL ROAD HALT   No platform or shelter, opened in 1912.

WORLE TOWN   Originally Worle, then Worle (Moor Lane) from 1913 and Worle Town 1917. Station building incorporated booking office and waiting room. An original low wooden platform was later removed; small wooden hut also provided shelter, In early days was permanently staffed; also a run-round loop and a siding into the gas works.

EBDON LANE HALT   Small wooden shelter provided but no platform; an early milk platform removed in the early 1930s.

WICK ST LAWRENCE   Originally a station but re-designated 'halt' in about 1928. The wooden station building was divided internally into a waiting room on the left and a booking hall to the right, the latter used primarily as a store.

HAM LANE HALT   Served local farming community (the milk platform comprised the base of an old wagon). There was a small wooden hut but no platform.

BROADSTONE HALT   Opened in 1927 with a very small sentry box type halt and no platform.

KINGSTON ROAD HALT   Largely served local farmers; milk platform in place until early 1930s. No platform but a small shelter provided.

COLEHOUSE LANE HALT   Served the local rural community with a long narrow shelter. In early 1939 shelter was replaced across the line when the original site was required for an access into a new BBC transmitter.

CLEVEDON   This was the Headquarters of the Railway with the Company Offices, locomotive shed, carriage shed and workshop. The principal building, with a semi-circular iron roof, incorporated a waiting room, booking office and toilets. A separate elevated platform with waiting shelter erected in 1919; water tank at either end. Modifications were made from the original layout when the second section to Portishead opened in 1907. A tight curved loop line provided a rarely used connection with the GWR Clevedon Branch. Today virtually all the station site is covered by the Safeway store car park.

CLEVEDON – PORTISHEAD
(All opened except one 7th August 1907)

CLEVEDON EAST HALT   Sited in the beauty spot of Swiss Valley; there was a wooden hut and a siding to a nearby joinery works.

CLEVEDON ALL SAINTS HALT   A basic facility with no platform or shelter opened in 1927 at this gated level crossing.

WALTON PARK HALT   No platform provided but a rustic style hut; a siding led into Conygar Quarry.

WALTON-IN-GORDANO HALT   Served this village in the Gordano Valley with a wooden shelter and no platform. Loop and cattle pens added in 1926.

CADBURY ROAD HALT   Primarily served the settlement of Weston-in-Gordano; name probably given to encourage visitors who could walk 1½ miles to the nearby Cadbury Camp. Only a hut provided.

CLAPTON ROAD HALT   Sited at a level crossing serving the village of Clapton-in-Gordano. No shelter provided.

PORTISHEAD SOUTH   Comprised a wooden shelter with no platform on the north east side of the line. A siding was used mainly by a coal merchant. The site is now within the housing area off Brampton Way.

PORTISHEAD   Originally had no platform; passengers using gravel surface at ground level; by 1920 a platform, twelve inches high, was erected. The original rustic single building with a wooden roof incorporated a waiting room and booking office; a later extension provided a separate ladies room. Beyond the station was a junction with the GWR branch line. The site of the station is now covered by the north west end of Wyndham Way.

Opposite page top Weston-super-Mare Ashcombe Road. A view east, the principal building to the left (behind the buffers); the elevated wooden platform with shelter (middle distance).

Opposite page centre Weston-super-Mare. The elevated platform and shelter with petrol car pictured in 1931.

Opposite page bottom Ebdon Road Halt. The small wooden shelter in December 1938.

Above Wick St Lawrence. Wooden shelter incorporating a waiting room and booking office, latter used primarily as a store. Photo taken in December 1938.

Left Ham Lane Halt. The small wooden hut in December 1938 looking towards Weston.

Below Broadstone Halt. A Clevedon to Weston train at the Halt in 1932.

Top left Kingston Road Halt. The small shelter looking towards Clevedon in December 1937.

Top right Colehouse Lane Halt. The long narrow shelter in its original position in December 1937 towards Clevedon.

Above Clevedon. Passengers waiting on the platform for the train to Weston arriving from Portishead on the Whit Bank Holiday 17th May 1937.

Left Clevedon. A view of 1921 towards Portishead of the main station building.

Above Clevedon East. Towards Portishead in 1938.

Left Walton Park. The rustic style shelter but no platform.

Opposite page top Cadbury Road. The Halt, serving Weston-in-Gordano, with a train for Portishead on the opening day of the Clevedon – Portishead section, 1907.

Opposite page bottom Portishead. A view on 7th August 1907 the opening day of the Clevedon – Portishead extension. The short station building prior to the later extension.

Below Walton-in-Gordano. Towards Portishead in 1938.

WEST SOMERSET MINERAL RAILWAY

In the 1850s the Brendon Hills, inland from Watchet, were the scene of major iron mining activity. In 1855 the West Somerset Mineral Railway (WSMR) was incorporated to connect the workings in the Hills to Watchet Harbour. A standard gauge line was opened between Watchet and Roadwater via Washford in April 1857 and the 7½ mile section to Comberow was completed by the end of 1857. Comberow lay at the foot of a one in four cable hauled incline which connected to further lines on the Hills. Although from early days passengers were carried on all sections of the Railway, these were largely miners and their families and the travel was unofficial, free and 'at their own risk'.

The WSMR decided to establish a full passenger service between Comberow and Watchet and the first official passenger train ran on 4th September 1865. In 1866 some 13,000 passengers were carried and by 1872 this number had risen to 19,000. Initially four passenger trains ran per day each way but this later reduced to two and then one. Stations were provided at Watchet, Washford, Roadwater and Comberow; some facilities at these places were provided ahead of the full passenger service.

The passenger service ceased on 7th November 1898. A short revival took place from 1907 and 1910 before final closure. Today the track alignment between Watchet and Washford is laid out as a walkway, 'The Old Mineral Line'.

Watchet. The site of the former station site photographed in August 1935 - the original two storey station master's house and offices (middle top) is in use today as flats, 'Old Station House'. The former stone goods shed and wooden goods shed survive (off left) as does the rear wall to the station platform (middle).

Above Washford. The WSMR station in September 1913, some three years after closure. The square stone building with a slate roof had a single platform. There was a siding but no loop line. No station remains survive today; a modern bungalow stands on the site.

Right Roadwater. A similar structure to that at Washford with one platform and a stone building. The derelict building shown in a *Railway Magazine* October 1934 photo. There goods sidings were provided with a coal platform between two of them. The station buildings and platform survive with an extension to form a bungalow.

Below Comberow. The engine 'Pontypool' with passenger coaches at the station in the 1870s. The station structure was similar to that at Washford and Roadwater. The station master's house stands at the foot of the incline. The house in the background survives but the station building was demolished in the 1930s. Traces of the platform remain.

FURTHER READING

Atthill R., *The Somerset & Dorset Railway*, David and Charles, 1967

Butt R.V.J., *Directory of Railway Stations*, Patrick Stephens, 1995

Clark R.H., *An Historical Survey of selected Great Western Railway Stations, Layouts and Illustrations*, Oxford Publishing Co. Volume 1 1976, Volume 2 1979, Volume 3, 1981

Clinker C.R., *Register of Closed Passenger Stations and Goods Depots 1830-1977*, Avon Anglia, 1978

Cubitt E., *West Somerset Railway Stations and Buildings*, West Somerset Railway,1994

Dale P., *Somerset's Lost Railways*, Stenlake Publishing, 2001

Deacon T., *The Somerset & Dorset : Aftermath of the Beeching Axe*, Oxford Publishing Co., 1995

Dowling G. and Whitehouse J., *British Railways Past and Present No. 16 Avon, Cotswolds and the Malverns*, Silver Link Publishing, 1993

Fry, P., *Railways into Wells*, Somerset and Dorset Railway Trust, 1998

Gosling, T. and Clement, M., *Somerset Railways*, Sutton Publishing, 2000

Hammond A., *S & D Memories*, Millstream Books, 1993

Harrison J.D., *The Bridgwater Railway*, Oakwood Press, 1990

Hawkins M., *Somerset & Dorset, Then and Now*, David and Charles, 1995

Hayes R., and Shaw M., *Railways in Wells*, HST, 1982/1986

Judge C.W. and Potts C.R., *Somerset and Dorset Railways : An Historical Survey of Track Layouts and Illustrations*, Oxford Publishing Co., 1979

Leigh C., *GWR Country Stations*, Ian Allan, Volume 1 1981/1985, Volume 2 1984

Leitch R., *The Railways of Keynsham*, RCTS, 1997

Madge R., *Railways around Exmoor*, The Exmoor Press, 1971/1975
Somerset Railways, The Dovecote Press, 1984

Maggs C.G., *Branch Lines of Somerset*, Alan Sutton, 1993
Bristol Railway Panorama, Millstream Books, 1990

GWR Bristol to Bath Line, Sutton Publishing, 2001

Highbridge in its Heyday, Oakwood Press, 1986

Mangotsfield to Bath Branch, Oakwood Press, 1992

Taunton Steam, Millstream Books, 1991

The Clevedon Branch, Wild Swan Publications, 1987

The Last Years of the Somerset & Dorset, Ian Allan, 1991

Weston, Clevedon & Portishead Railway, Oakwood Press, 1964

Maggs C.G., and Beale G., *The Camerton Branch*, Wild Swan Publications, 1985

Mitchell D., *British Railways Past and Present No 30 Somerset*, Past and Present Publishing Ltd, 1996

Mitchell V. and Smith K., Middleton Press (various publication dates)
Bath Green Park to Bristol, 1999
Bath to Evercreech Junction, 1988
Bournemouth to Evercreech Junction, 1987
Branch Line to Cheddar, 1997
Branch Lines around Chard and Yeovil, 1999
Branch Line to Minehead, 1990
Burnham to Evercreech Junction, 1989
Frome to Bristol, 1986
Salisbury to Yeovil, 1992
Taunton to Barnstaple, 1995
Taunton to Exeter, 2002
Westbury to Bath, 1995
Westbury to Taunton, 2002
Yeovil to Dorchester, 1990
Yeovil to Exeter, 1991

Peters I., *The Somerset & Dorset*, Oxford Publishing Co., 1974

Phillips D., *Steaming through the Cheddar Valley*, Ian Allan, 2002
Westbury to Weymouth Line, Oxford Publishing Co., 1994
Working Yeovil to Taunton Steam, Fox and Co., 1991

Phillips D., and Pryer G., *Salisbury to Exeter Line*, Oxford Publishing Co., 1997

Phillips D., and Eaton-Lacey R., *Working on the Chard Branch*, Fox and Co., 1991

Potts, C., *An Historical Survey of Selected Great Western Railway Stations, Layouts and Illustrations*, Oxford Publishing Co., Volume 4, 1985

Robertson K., *Great Western Railway Halts*, Volume 1 Irwell Press, 1990
Somerset and Avon Railways in Old Photographs, Alan Sutton, 1990

Sellick R., *The Old Mineral Line*, The Exmoor Press, 1981

Smith M., *The Railways of Bristol & Somerset*, Ian Allan, 1992

Strange P., *Weston, Clevedon & Portishead Railway*, Twelveheads Press, 1989

Thomas D.St.J., *Regional History of the Railways of Great Britain*, Volume 1 The West Country, David and Charles, 1981

Vaughan A., *Great Western Architecture : A Pictorial Record*, Oxford Publishing Co.,1977
GWR Junction Stations, Ian Allan, 1988

Vincent M., *Reflections on the Portishead Branch*, Oxford Publishing Co., 1983
Through Countryside & Coalfield, Oxford Publishing Co., 1990

ACKNOWLEDGEMENTS

The author is very grateful for the permission received to use photographs from the following collections: Lens of Sutton (inc photographs of the 1950s and 1960s taken by J.L. Smith, the owner of Lens of Sutton); pages 10 (top), 13 (top), 22, 23, 24, 25, 26, 27 (bottom), 30, 31, 37, 43, 46 (bottom), 47, 49 (top), 50, 53, 56, 62, 67, 68, 69 (bottom), 70, 71, 72, 75, 77, 78 (bottom), 80, 81, 83, 86, 87(top), 92 (bottom), 94 (top), 97 (top left), 99, 101, 104, 106, 113, 114, 120, 121 (top), 125, 127, 128 (top), 138, 139 (top), 143 (top), 145, 146, 147: Colin Caddy; pages 12, 13 (bottom), 48, 51 (bottom), 63, 66, 82, 108 (top), 109 (top), 110 (top left) 116 (middle), 118 (top), 122 (top), 122 (bottom), 129, 136 (top), 144: Colin Maggs; pages 4, 17, 54 (top), 55, 78 (top), 79 (top), 89, 102 (top), 133 (top): Mike Tozer; pages 15 (bottom), 35 (top), 54 (bottom), 92, 97 (top right), 98, 105 (top), 119, 128 (bottom), 136 (bottom), 140, 155: National Railway Museum/LGRP Collection; pages 5, 21 (bottom), 27 (top), 28, 38 (top), 61 (top), 73 (bottom), 84 (top), 93 (bottom), 100, 121 (bottom), 139 (middle): Brunel University Mowat Collection (W.R. Burton); pages 33, 45, 58: Joe Moss (via Roger Carpenter); pages 35 (bottom), 42, 52, 79 (bottom), 84 (bottom), 94 (bottom), 134, 141: P.J. Garland (via Roger Carpenter); pages 40, 91, 118 (bottom): Roger Carpenter; pages 36, 137, 148: R.C. Riley/The Transport Treasury; pages 44, 59, 60, 69 (top), 102 (bottom): E.T. Gill (via R.K. Blencowe); pages 41 (top), 87 (bottom), 90: Michael Hale; pages 19, 20, 21 (top): Hugh Ballantyne; page 57: North Somerset Museum; page 130: North Somerset Library and Information Service; page 131 (top and bottom): Joannes Publications; page 105 (bottom): Twelveheads Press and Peter Strange; pages 151 (bottom), 152 (middle and bottom), 153 (top left, top right, middle), 154 (top, middle, bottom).

The remaining photographs were taken by the author or are from his own collection where the copyright owner is unknown or unclear. Prints from the Brunel University Transport collection are available from W.R. Burton, 3 Fairway, Clifton, York YO30 5QA.